ZORBA'S PARTHENON

A TAVERNA BY THE SEA

PETER BARBER

Zorba's Parthenon: A Taverna by the Sea

First published in 2025

Copyright © Peter Barber, 2025

The moral right of Peter Barber to be identified as the author of this work has been asserted in accordance with the Copyright, Designs and Patents Act of 1988.

All rights reserved. No part of this publication may be reproduced, stored in a retrieval system, or transmitted in any form or by any means, electronic, mechanical, photocopying, recording, or otherwise, without the prior permission of the copyright owner.

Paperback ISBN: 978-1-916574-23-6

Hardback ISBN: 978-1-916574-24-3

Cover Design and Formatting by Kathleen Harryman
https://www.kathleenharryman.co.uk

SCAN THE QR CODE FOR MORE
INFORMATION ABOUT
PETER BARBER AND HIS BOOKS.

BOOKS BY PETER BARBER:

THE PARTHENON SERIES:
A Parthenon on our Roof
A Parthenon in Pefki
The Parthenon Paradox

THE MUSINGS SERIES:
Musings from a Greek Village
Musings from a Pandemic

Contents

Introduction: *A Memoir with a View and a Pinch of Salt* 13

Chapter One: *The Illusion of Peace* 15

Chapter Two: *The Great Fish Paradox* 32

Chapter Three: *The Five-Metre Rule and the Fall of Zorba* 39

Chapter Four: *Mourning in the Village* 49

Chapter Five: *Convincing Zorba* 61

Chapter Six: *Zorba - The Man, the Myth, the Menu* 66

Chapter Seven: *Partners in Crime (and Tsipouro)* 71

Chapter Eight: *Building the Dream (and Other Poor Decisions)* 79

Chapter Nine: *Lemons, Wine, and Other Disasters* 84

Chapter Ten: *The (Not So) Soft Opening* 95

Interlude: *Part 1 - On Love and Alex* 104

Chapter Eleven: *The Whispering Trees* 109

Chapter Twelve: *The Cheese Stands Alone* 16

Chapter Thirteen: *Katerina the Goat* 122

Chapter Fourteen: *Enter the Matriarch* 126

Chapter Fifteen: *Dimitri and the Church of Storms*..................132

Chapter Sixteen: *The Grand Reopening (Take Two)*..................142

Chapter Seventeen: *The Morning After*..................152

Chapter Eighteen: *Spiros and the Tobacco Police*..................156

Chapter Nineteen: *Dimitri's Big Idea*..................163

Chapter Twenty: *Mary Of the Plates Or "The Reason Half the Village Suddenly Needed More Bread"*..................170

Chapter Twenty-On: *The Man from the Municipality (and the Goat)*.176

Chapter Twenty-Two: *Diplomacy in Hooves*..................181

Chapter Twenty-Three: *The Letter*..................184

Chapter Twenty-Four: *Vassiliki The Baker from Heaven*..................187

Chapter Twenty-Five: *Don't Mess with the Bench*..................92

Interlude: *Part 2 - On Learning to Be Greek*..................99

Chapter Twenty-Six: *Part 2 - On Learning to Be Greek*..................203

Chapter Twenty-Seven: *Influence This*..................208

Chapter Twenty-Eight: *The Tourist Invasion*..................214

Chapter Twenty-Nine: *Hooves and Whiskers*..................218

Chapter Thirty: *Who Owns the Lemons?*..................227

Chapter Thirty-One: *The Fish Festival Disaster*..................232

Chapter Thirty-Two: *Among the Lemons*..................238

Chapter Thirty-Three: *Exit Strategies and Scratched Surfaces*..................243

Chapter Thirty-Four: *The Money Bit (Unfortunately)*..................248

Chapter Thirty-Five: *Holy Smoke, He's Got a Rocket Launcher*..........254

Chapter Thirty-Six: *Ghosts of the Grove*..........260

Chapter Thirty-Seven: *A Name Day to Remember*..........265

Chapter Thirty-Eight: *Strangers at the Gate*..........274

Chapter Thirty-Nine: *The Great Tsipouro War*..........279

Chapter Forty: *Father Evangelos vs. the Octopus*..........287

Chapter Forty-One: *Claude's Cultural Coup*..........292

Chapter Forty-Two: *Marmite and Mayhem*..........299

Chapter Forty-Three: *How to Start a Religious Schism with a Teabag*..........306

Chapter Forty-Four: *Alex's Aunt from Athens*..........312

Chapter Forty-Five: *Zorba's Dream*..........317

Chapter Forty-Six: *The Offer*..........321

Chapter Forty-Seven: *Why is the Goat Wearing a Badge?*..........329

Chapter Forty-Eight: *Zorba's Answe*..........336

Chapter Forty-Nine: *A Place to Belong*..........341

Chapter Fifty: *Under the Lemon Moon*..........344

Chapter Fifty-One: *A Parthenon by the Sea*..........348

Epilogue: *After the Storm*..........351

ZORBA'S TAVERNA - THE TROUBLE WITH GOATS & MAYORS -

EPISODE 2

Chapter One: *The Invasion of the Spoon-Wielding Matriarchs*..........356

Acknowledgements: *A Goat, a Godmother, and The Girl Who Made It All Possible Now raise your glass*..367

About the Author..373

ZORBA'S PARTHENON

A TAVERNA BY THE SEA

PETER BARBER

INTRODUCTION

A Memoir with a View and a Pinch of Salt

This book is a memoir. Mostly.

It began, as many Greek stories do, with good intentions, a strong breeze, and a small Greek fishing village where we found our home. It's based on real places, real people, and real events, though some of them might argue otherwise (especially the people).

Names have been changed, stories nudged, and a few details given a fresh coat of paint. Not to mislead, but to protect the innocent, and, more importantly, to keep things interesting. Because let's be honest: if you want hard facts, you'd try an instruction manual. This is a book about Greece. Which means the truth is flexible, the coffee is strong, and everyone has an opinion.

Think of it as a taverna by the sea. Some of the chairs wobble. The menu is written in three languages (none of them spelled quite right), and the cat you thought belonged to the owner has actually been living there longer than he has.

So, yes, it's a memoir. But with a bit of driftwood fiction floating in. A few myths wrapped in meze. A splash of exaggeration, like too much oil on a Greek salad. And if something in here didn't technically happen exactly the way I tell it, I promise it should have.

Welcome to Zorba's taverna.

Pull up a chair. The table's probably uneven. But the view? That's all true.

CHAPTER ONE

THE ILLUSION OF PEACE

When I first arrived in Greece, I tried my hardest to adapt. I learned to order coffee, nod knowingly when people said *"kala"* (good), and even managed to avoid crashing the car into anything stationary for nearly three weeks. I considered this progress.

But to *be* Greek? That's something else entirely.

You don't become Greek by signing forms or marrying one (although, admittedly, that helps). You become Greek the way olives become oil. Through time, pressure, and a bit of chaos.

It's not about language. My Greek is still a creative work in progress. I once asked for a receipt and accidentally suggested someone's grandmother was a pigeon. No one batted an eye. They just nodded and brought me a biscuit.

And it's not about paperwork. In fact, the more paperwork you fill in, the less Greek you feel. Greeks treat forms the way they treat bad weather: with exasperation, resignation, and a firm belief that ignoring it might make it go away.

No, to be Greek is to live with a kind of joyful resistance. To rules. To schedules. To silence. To the idea that anything should ever be simple. It's sitting down for coffee and standing up three hours later having planned a revolution, rearranged three weddings, and discussed the price of tomatoes in five regions. It's calling someone your cousin even if you're not technically related, but you did both go to school with Manoli's second wife's sister. It's understanding that time is flexible. "Now" means soon. "Soon" means later. "Later" means tomorrow. And "tomorrow" means possibly in spring. It's accepting that your neighbours will know what you had for dinner before you've finished chewing. It's arguing passionately, loudly, and with flailing arms, and then, two minutes later, hugging, laughing, and passing the wine.

It's mistrusting politicians, loving your *yiayia* more than God, and believing, deep down, that no meal is complete without feta, no solution is complete without shouting, and no problem is so big that it can't be temporarily ignored by going for a swim.

Alex taught me most of this without meaning to.

She never tried to make me Greek. She struggled a little to get rid of some of my English reserve. But she simply *was* Greek. Gloriously, unapologetically so. And by standing beside her, I slowly, awkwardly, and quite possibly illegally, became a little bit Greek myself.

Two decades in, and I now gesture when I speak. I mistrust any officialdom that works too efficiently. I've learned the difference between good *tsipouro* and the kind that can remove paint from doors. I've danced badly at name days, been kissed by strangers at funerals, and learned to accept that plans are merely ideas with a time attached.

So, no – I wasn't born Greek.

But I am something else now. Something in between. Not quite tourist, not quite native. A half-sunburnt hybrid with one foot in British understatement and the other in Greek outrage.

And honestly? It's the best thing I've ever been.

***

After England, with its dignified drizzle and small, controlled explosions of emotional repression, I thought I was ready for something more truly Greek; something simpler; more elemental. Something that didn't involve spreadsheets or queueing to make an appointment to join a queue.

But where we had settled was Glyfada. Glyfada was once a sleepy coastal suburb of Athens where chickens outnumbered cars and a polite wave could get you through any road junction, but in recent years it had grown up, developed and become a bustling city. It had put on heels and expensive sunglasses and became the Athenian Riviera.

The transformation had been gradual, but relentless. There were designer shops now, their names elegantly French, their prices pointedly international. They sold very small items in very small bags with very large prices on the tags. It was the sort of place where you left the shop wondering if perhaps you had accidentally purchased a lease on the window display.

But it wasn't just the shops that had changed. The roads had changed too. The dusty tracks we used to stroll down in sandals were now slick ribbons of black tarmac. They now had lanes. And signs. And, most controversially of all, traffic lights, blinking with bureaucratic optimism.

Greek drivers in general took this new development with a shrug. The lights, while technically in use, were regarded more as suggestions than commandments. People would sometimes stop, but usually only if there was someone watching. A police car. A stern-looking grandmother. A German tourist with a camera. Otherwise, a red light was treated like a particularly strong rumour: interesting, but unconfirmed.

And zebra crossings? Ah, the zebra crossings, painted across roads with great ceremony and absolutely no purpose. No one in Greece, driver or pedestrian, has ever fully grasped their meaning. To most locals, they are decorative flourishes, possibly left over from a half-finished art installation. Aesthetically pleasing, yes, but functionally about as useful as a chocolate radiator.

You can always spot a tourist in Athens by the way they step onto a zebra crossing expecting cars to stop. They walk out confidently, arms swinging, eyes trusting. There is a moment, just one, when they realise nothing is slowing down, least of all the scooter currently aiming directly for their kneecaps. And then, in a flash of survival instinct, they leap back onto the pavement, clutching their Lonely Planet and muttering something about public transport.

The locals, meanwhile, simply dart between cars wherever the shade is.

Alex had grown up just up the road in Athens, a city where conversations echo off balconies, politics is personal, and lunch is a contact sport. Her childhood was steeped in the hum of *bouzouki* music, the clatter of cutlery, and the kind of opinions that arrive fully formed and loudly expressed.

I'd been absorbed into her family like a curious foreign exchange student, adopted and occasionally roasted, not unkindly, for my lack of Greek and the fact that I was, in their words, "very pale but sweet".

I was regularly told I was too thin. Not behind my back, of course – that would have been impolite. No, this information was delivered directly to my face, across tables groaning under the weight of stuffed vine leaves, *spanakopita*, grilled meats, and deep familial concern.

My mother-in-law, Debbie, was the ringleader of this nutritional intervention. A force of nature in an apron, she could simultaneously prepare three courses, call four cousins, critique the Prime Minister, and sing a melancholy Greek love song, all while keeping one eye on whether or not I had touched the *moussaka*.

She would press food into my hands with the urgency of someone saving a life. Saying no was not an option. Saying "I'm full" was seen as a medical emergency. Refusing seconds was treated as an insult to her lineage and possibly the entire region of Athens.

And then, often in the very next breath, she would eye my stomach with grave suspicion.

"Peteraki," she'd say, folding her arms as only a mother-in-law can, "you're getting fat. This is not healthy. Who will look after my daughter when I die? You must lose some weight."

It was less a comment and more a diagnosis. A life prognosis. A call to action, preferably involving herbal tea, walking, and fewer fried things.

So I existed in a strange culinary paradox. Caught between being dangerously underfed and suspiciously bloated, often within the same meal.

I learned quickly that in Greece, food is not just sustenance. It's affection, it's diplomacy, it's a battlefield. And whatever size you are, you're probably doing it wrong. But I had survived it. Just.

So after the mayhem of city life in Glyfada, where arguments about coffee could escalate to family courtroom levels of drama, we were desperate for something slower. Quieter. Less combustible. Something where conversations didn't involve shouting over the noise of the aircraft taking off from the nearby Athens airport, or of my mother-in-law Debbie's exchanges with her neighbours up and down the street at the volume of a pneumatic road breaker. No, we needed to relax for a while, kick back and find the real Greece.

So, we left the traffic-fumed air of Glyfada, and went in search of old Greece.

When we stumbled across Telios, it felt like a mirage. A fishing village at the far northern tip of the island of Evia, tucked between pine-covered hills and a sea so blue it looked Photoshopped. The kind of place no one really talks about, because they'd rather keep it a secret.

There were no traffic lights. Not because of some municipal oversight, but because they simply weren't needed. The locals knew exactly what time the farmer would be pulling his tractor out of the field into the road. When the shepherd would be bringing his sheep around a blind bend. Rush hour consisted of one donkey, two mopeds, and a man with a wheelbarrow full of courgettes.

We were enchanted. Who wouldn't be? The sky stretched wide, the air was thick with pine and salt and thyme, and the loudest sound was the rhythmic creaking of a fishing boat nudging against the dock. The village dog, known to everyone and owned by no one, barked thoughtfully at birds, tourists, and sometimes at the sea itself.

We breathed. We walked. We swam. We said smug things like, "This is it. This is our forever peace."

So, of course, we built a house.

We bought a plot of land. The sort of plot you could only fully understand if you held the plans upside down and squinted into the sun. Most of it was covered in brambles and bamboo, and even the land registry had no idea of the size, and it had completely missed the river running along the back. Then we hired a builder named Stamos, who, despite his deadlines existing in a separate dimension from ours, created our dream home: a modest palace with a terrace for dramatic sunsets, and a view of the sea that could make a cynic weep.

We called it Telios Palace. Not out of grandeur, but necessity. There was no address, no named street, no helpful numbering system. We were often forced to tell delivery drivers we lived "fifty metres past where Illias the barrel maker lives, opposite where the donkey usually sits." This worked. Usually.

Finally, we were going to relax. Retire. Fade gracefully into the background like a couple of sun-dried figs. We had moved to Telios for the peace. That had been the plan, anyway. The noble, delusional plan.

And then, as with all plans in Greece, reality arrived like a donkey wandering into your kitchen. The Greek gods decided to test us.

What no one tells you about Greek villages is that "peaceful" does not mean "quiet". It means "communal". It means your life is now public property. It means you will be loved, included, interrogated, judged, fed, celebrated, and occasionally dragged into a village feud over whose cat fathered which kittens.

Life in a Greek village is a bit like joining an amateur theatre group without auditioning. Everyone has a role, and you find yourself cast whether you like it or not. Over time, we got to know the key players:

Zorba – The taverna owner. Half-man, half-grumble. Built of salt, cigarette smoke, and the kind of stubbornness that can stop time. If the village is a ship, he's the weathered captain who insists he's retired, but still checks the rigging every morning.

Theodora – Our unofficial village matriarch and culinary enforcer. Her food is legend, her eyebrows terrifying, and her opinion on parsley in *moussaka* is enough to start a war.

George – Cheesemaker and reluctant handyman and husband to Theodora. Spends half his time making cheese, the other half denying he promised to fix anything. Speaks only when necessary. Usually when Theodora lets him.

Mary – Theodora's daughter. Beautiful, bold, and fully aware of it; grace with a side of sarcasm. She can carry six plates and silence six arguments at once, all without smudging her lipstick.

Dimitri – Fisherman, hunter, plumber, part-time philosopher. Possibly immortal. Frequently appears with octopuses, rabbits, or suspicious "herbs" he swears are oregano.

Maria – The gossip oracle. News arrives in the village via three sources: the post, the priest, and Maria (usually first). If something happened, she knows. If it didn't, she's already invented a better version.

Claude – Our French friend. Moved here for the sun, stayed for the poetry. Wears linen even in December, and has attempted to introduce jazz nights three times. Each attempt was politely buried beneath a mountain of baklava.

Stamos – Builder. Craftsman. Occasionally found constructing things no one asked for. Once built a bread oven during a conversation about repainting a wall. If you tell him not to, he will. Twice.

Eleni – Bureaucracy-whisperer. Speaks fluent government. Fills in forms faster than most people read them. Can smell an inspector approaching from a kilometre away.

Father Evangelos – The village priest. Quiet. Kind. Possibly descended from a cloud. Blesses everything from baptisms to fridge repairs. Never raises his voice but can silence a room by adjusting his glasses.

Spiros – The oldest man in the village. Possibly the oldest man in Greece. Has smoked since the invention of tobacco. Drinks *tsipouro* like it's sacramental wine. Hasn't changed routine since 1963, and doesn't intend to.

And then, of course, there's **Alex**.

The reason we're here. The reason *I* am here.
The reason there's a Parthenon on our roof and lemon trees growing where logic used to live.
To the villagers, Alex is still "the Athenian", which, in rural Greece, is basically a polite way of saying *foreign.* Never mind that she spoke the local dialect like she'd been born under a Telios fig tree. Or that she picked olives with the speed and scowl of a seasoned harvester. Or that she once out-argued Eleni *and* the electricity man in the same afternoon, and still got him to waive the reconnection fee.

None of that made her a villager.

Not officially.

Not yet.

Alex doesn't just live in the village. She *bends* it. Gently, firmly, and with a smile that suggests she's already four steps ahead of you. She has the soul of a poet, the energy of a caffeinated olive picker, and the unshakeable conviction that anything is possible, especially if *she* says it is.

She once decided we should build a house.

So we did.

She once wanted a Parthenon on the roof.

So I built one. Got arrested. Then built it again, legally this time.

She remembers birthdays. She brings cake. She listens when others pretend not to hear. And somehow, she convinces bureaucrats, builders, and grumpy fishermen to say yes when their default is no.

She's fierce when she needs to be. Kind when no one's watching. And absolutely terrifying in ways that can't be explained, only survived.

And yet, beneath it all, she's joy. Not the loud, theatrical kind. The quiet, steady sort that grows things. Friendships. Projects. Hope.

She's the centre of my world.

And, increasingly, the unofficial mayor of this village.

Now, she wants to change the village. Not dramatically.

Not loudly. But in the quiet way someone opens a window and lets in a breeze.

Our evening strolls became diplomatic missions. Alex would pause to compliment Theodora's tomatoes, check in on George's goats, and reassure Maria, again, that we weren't childless. (Our children had grown up and lived somewhere else. This made no sense to Maria. Her youngest was 52, and he still lived at home. She would always ignore us, though; because she couldn't see our children, they obviously didn't exist, so we must be cursed.)

There were name days to remember, olive oil rivalries to carefully sidestep, and an uncanny number of opportunities to be accidentally absorbed into village life. One afternoon I was handed a paintbrush and ended up repainting the wall of a tiny chapel alongside three elderly men and a dog that appeared to be in charge. Another time, I was somehow appointed judge of a *tsipouro*-making competition, despite having no real palate, no formal training, and a distinct lack of survival instincts. By the third sample, I could no longer feel my face. By the fifth, I was fluent in Ancient Greek and may have declared someone's donkey the winner. Alex found me under a fig tree hours later, still holding the scorecards and arguing with a potted basil plant about ethics.

The aim, though, was always clear to Alex. She didn't want to change the village itself – just our place in it. She wanted to turn us from outsiders into honorary locals, or at the very least, tolerated oddities. If we were ever going to make a real life here, she said, we'd need allies, invitations, and possibly someone who'd loan us a goat in times of need. This was diplomacy, Greek village-style. Less about politics, more about pies.

And then there was the taverna.

Zorba's taverna.

At first, we thought we'd just be customers. Casual visitors, just two new faces in the breeze. A little ouzo here, a grilled sardine there. Maybe some mild eavesdropping if things got interesting.

But the taverna had plans of its own. Slowly, subtly, it pulled us in. Not just as diners, but as characters in the story. The taverna, like the village itself, didn't want bystanders. It wanted participants.

It stood, as all good Greek tavernas should, at the very end of the road. Past the last turning, beyond the leaning mailbox, just before the sea runs out of patience.

Not a place you stumbled upon.

A place you arrived at.

Because you meant to.

It wasn't large. Or symmetrical. Or in any way fashionable. The walls had once been white; now they were the colour of sea salt and old stories. The roof sloped gently in a direction no one could quite agree on. There was a door, and also a curtain. Most locals ignored the door. The curtain had a certain flair.

To the front, a corrugated tin roof covered a patchwork of

tables and chairs, none of which matched. Some leaned. Some creaked. All were fiercely defended by the locals who'd sat in them since the fall of the drachma. Out front, a few bold tables teetered on the beach itself, wedged just above the tide line, their legs buried like stubborn roots in the sand.

This was where Zorba held court.

Zorba ran the taverna alone. Not because he was lonely, but because no one else would dare.

He was the host, the waiter, the cook, and the bartender. Though "bartending" often meant uncorking whatever bottle he had closest and pouring with the solemnity of a saint.

His menu was verbal. His rules were fluid. His food was… fine. If you didn't ask too many questions. If you liked sardines. And if you understood that portion sizes were decided by mood, not mathematics. The *tzatziki* had enough garlic to stun a goat at twenty paces.

Ordering was an art. You didn't ask for what you wanted; you asked what Zorba had.

Sometimes it was *moussaka*, mostly it was sardines. Sometimes it was a shrug and a cigarette and a loaf of bread dropped silently on your table like a parable.

The drinks came in small glasses, sometimes clean, always generous. You'd get bottled beer if you were lucky, something unlabelled and flammable if you weren't. The *tsipouro* came in miniature bottles, the kind you'd expect to see on an airline or smuggled out of duty free. Zorba refilled them himself, out of a battered copper still that lurked in the back room next to a pile of fishing nets and a calendar from 1997. Nobody asked too many questions about that either.

Step through the doorway (or push the curtain) and you'd find the kitchen: part workshop, part shrine. A gas burner. A chipped sink. Shelves bowed with pots and tins. A pan that had survived three generations and one small explosion. And a chalkboard that simply read, "No Substitutions. No Complaints. No Problem."

Behind the kitchen were two small rooms: one for storage, one possibly for hiding when tourists got too enthusiastic. Both smelled of lemons, onions, and a long, slow simmering of time.

There was a fridge, but it wasn't always plugged in. There was a till, but it wasn't ever used.

There was a receipt book, but no one knew where it lived.

Zorba's wasn't quaint. It was *particular*.

It had no website, no card machine, and no sense of time. Service arrived when it arrived. Conversation, however, was instant, whether you wanted it or not.

It was the sort of place where a dog might wander through, followed by a fisherman, followed by a debate about fishing quotas that ended with a toast and a small plate of olives. There was no music. Just the soft scrape of cutlery, the hum of cicadas, and the ever-present sound of the sea trying to join the conversation.

And before we knew it, we weren't sitting at the edge of

the story any more. We were in it. We were no longer outsiders. We were "Peter and Alex". A unit. An Anglo–Greek experiment in domestic diplomacy. Regulars. Trusted faces. Included in everything from impromptu political debates to last-minute baptisms and, occasionally, acts of mild legal ambiguity.

After five years in Telios, we had survived three floods, several storms of biblical proportion, and one forest fire that nearly wiped out the village, and we had been arrested due to a complaint from a grumpy neighbour who claimed our garden had blocked the river and caused the village to flood. (It hadn't, of course, the river had simply changed course during the storm. But the photograph he produced was both convincing and dramatic. Our floodlights, once at the edge of the garden, now sat in the middle of a newly invented river. It looked damning if you didn't know where the river used to be.)

So, no. The village of Telios wasn't peaceful. But it was alive.

Messy, unpredictable, loudly affectionate, hilariously frustrating, impossibly generous. A place where one day you're arguing about parking sheep, and the next you're holding hands under the stars while the village orchestra, such as it is, tunes up for an impromptu music night in the taverna.

And somehow, that suited us perfectly. Because peace, as it turns out, is overrated.

But purpose? Connection? Community? A never-ending supply of home-brewed *tsipouro*?

That's paradise.

Chapter Two

The Great Fish Paradox

The taverna in Greece is not just a place you go to eat. It's where life happens. Loudly, slowly, with too much wine and not nearly enough logic, or, sometimes, far too much. It's the centre of the village. The beating heart. The accidental theatre of everyday philosophy combined with real life.

In ancient Greece, the philosophers taught in the agora, the marketplace beneath the Acropolis. They'd wander around in togas, stroking beards and asking questions like, "What is virtue?" and "How do we live a good life?" Or "I know that I know nothing… but I'm pretty sure it was your turn to buy the wine."

These days, the questions have shifted slightly. Now they sound more like, "If the *souvlaki* falls on the floor, was it meant to fall? Should I eat it anyway?" Or, "If the waiter brings one more carafe of wine... and I order two more... how many will I deny drinking tomorrow?"

But don't be fooled. The thinking hasn't stopped. It's just moved locations. The agora is now the taverna. The Acropolis has been replaced by a cracked patio with uncomfortable wicker chairs and a view of the sea. Socrates, if he were alive today, would absolutely be sitting under the vine-covered pergola arguing about whether the octopus is better grilled or stewed.

This is where the real conversations happen. The bold political theories. The arguments about fishing rights and football tactics. The passionate debate over whether Yiannis actually caught that fish himself or got it from his cousin in the next village. You don't need a podium or a scroll to share your philosophy, just a glass of *retsina* and an opinion you're willing to shout over everyone else.

And the beauty is, nobody agrees. Ever. Which is exactly the point. Because in the Greek taverna, disagreement isn't rude, it's a sport. Voices are raised, arms are waved, tables are thumped. And then someone pours more wine and brings out the olives and everyone carries on like nothing happened. This, I think, is a true civilisation.

***

It was spring in Telios, and the village was getting ready for the season.

The tourists had begun to arrive, along with the inflatable flamingos they dragged to the sea, but the thrumming confusion of summer had yet to invade us. The locals were free to claim their streets, their beaches, and most importantly, their tables at the taverna. The cafés were still empty, the chairs inviting.

And so I found myself at my favourite spot on the beach, outside Zorba's taverna, sipping a coffee as the boats swayed lazily in the water, the sea whispering secrets to the shore.

A fisherman tended to his nets nearby, his hands moving with the practiced ease of a man who knows his craft. Not far off, a lone swimmer carved gentle circles in the bay, his movements as meditative as they were deliberate. Overhead, seagulls perched on the rocks, feigning indifference but keeping a sharp eye on the fishermen below.

Life was gentle here. Unrushed. Strangely profound.

Yet today, my attention was drawn not to the sea, or the hills, or the impossible blueness of the sky, but to the table beside mine, where a very Greek argument was brewing.

Adonis, a man whose name was almost as grand as his ego, stood with arms crossed, a smirk playing at the corners of his mouth, and his canvas waders still damp from the morning's work. His skin, bronzed by years of sun and salt, seemed to glow with the confidence of a man who had never lost an argument – at least, not one he acknowledged. Beside him was Dimitri.

Dimitri is the kind of man who appears exactly when you need him, and just as mysteriously disappears when you don't. Dimitri looks like he's been carved out of driftwood and stubbornness. His wardrobe seems to consist entirely of battered trousers, mismatched shirts, and the occasional impressive hat rescued from unknown origins.

Officially, he's a fisherman. Unofficially, he's an odd-job man, a part-time hunter, a sometime plumber, a semi-professional *tsipouro*-brewer. No one knows exactly how Dimitri earns a living. He seems to exist outside the normal rules of employment, appearing with a bucket of fish one day, a wild boar leg the next. But today he had trodden on forbidden ground – at least according to Adonis.

"Those are my fish," Adonis declared, jabbing a calloused finger towards the bucket at Dimitri's feet. "You only caught them because of me. We should split them; half for you, half for me."

Dimitri raised an eyebrow, amused.

"Your fish, Adonis? They seem quite happy in my bucket."

Adonis waved a dismissive hand, as though this was a minor detail.

"Without my boat, you'd have caught nothing. The fish gather because of me. It's simple cause and effect."

Now, to the untrained eye, this might have seemed like a squabble over a few unlucky sardines. But in Greece, nothing is ever that simple. This wasn't just an argument; this was a philosophical debate.

To understand Adonis's logic, you needed to know his routine. Each morning, he anchored his boat just outside the harbour after a long night of trawling. His crew, efficient and surly, cleaned the catch, tossing scraps into the sea. It was a buffet, and the fish knew it. Where there are scraps, there are fish. And where there are fish… there are fishermen.

Dimitri included.

He had learned to time his outings around this routine. Why waste petrol cruising the bay when you could anchor beside Adonis and let the fish come to you?

Lines would be dipped into the water, and within minutes, the hooks would be heavy with fish who had mistaken their final meal for breakfast.

Adonis, standing proudly on the deck of his boat, had never been fond of this opportunism.

He watched in dignified silence every morning, until today, when Dimitri's bucket filled up faster than his temper could hold.

"You see," Adonis continued, leaning back with the air of a man about to deliver a lecture at the Academy of Athens, "I am the cause. Without me, there is no effect. Ergo, half those fish are mine."

Dimitri rubbed his chin thoughtfully, as though he were considering a serious theorem rather than a claim of fish-ownership-by-proximity.

Zorba's Parthenon - A Taverna by the Sea

"So, let me get this straight," he said. "I pay for the petrol. I cast the line. I reel in the fish. And you deserve half just for... existing?"

Adonis nodded solemnly. "Exactly."

It was the kind of logic that would have Socrates reaching for his cup of hemlock.

In fact, I imagined the ancient philosophers sitting at the next table, watching with keen interest.

Plato would stroke his beard and muse on the nature of ownership.

Aristotle might lecture Adonis on the difference between potentiality and actuality.

Zeno of Elea, ever the troublemaker, would probably point out that Adonis's claim was a paradox: a man who didn't fish, but who claimed the catch.

Dimitri, however, didn't need ancient philosophy. He had simplicity and sarcasm on his side.

"If your boat is so magical," he said, "perhaps you should cast a line yourself, instead of staring into your coffee."

The two men continued, voices rising and falling like the tide. To an outsider, it might have seemed heated, even hostile. But underneath, there was humour. An old, stubborn, affectionate humour.

This is how villagers bond here: not over agreement, but over disagreement. Not over winning, but over the pleasure of the battle. It's not about the fish. It's about the argument.

The back-and-forth that sharpens minds, strengthens friendships, and reminds everyone that life, like fishing, is best approached with patience, stubbornness, and a healthy respect for the absurd.

As the sun climbed higher, casting silver across the sea, the argument began to dissolve into laughter. Adonis threw up his hands in mock defeat, demanding that Dimitri buy him a glass of ouzo as compensation for "emotional distress".

And just like that, the great fish feud was over. Until tomorrow. Because in the taverna, there is no final victory, there is only the joy of arguing well and living better.

In many ways, the taverna is our modern-day Parthenon. A little faded, a little chaotic, missing a few tiles, but still standing. Still beautiful in its glorious imperfection. It may not be a temple to the gods, but it's certainly a temple to the good life. A shared plate of calamari, a warm breeze off the sea, and the knowledge that someone will eventually bring the bill, possibly next week.

This is the world of the seaside taverna. It's not just about the food or the views (though both are excellent), but the people, the madness, the stories, the arguments about fish, whose olives are best, where the best cheese comes from. It's a tribute to Greece as it actually is: unpredictable, generous, hilarious, and occasionally held together with string and goodwill.

And if you're looking for answers, don't expect straight ones. The Parthenon didn't have straight lines either. That's the charm.

CHAPTER THREE

THE FIVE-METRE RULE AND THE FALL OF ZORBA

Zorba had finally decided to close the taverna.

Not because he'd run out of customers – people still came, locals and tourists alike, lured by the scent of grilled sardines and the promise of a decent sunset. Not because he was tired of the work – though he did occasionally mutter that he was too old to be arguing with fishermen at 6 a.m. about the price of calamari. No, the last straw was something far more absurd.

It happened on a Tuesday. These things always do.

The sun was high, the sea was calm, and the octopus hanging on the line outside Zorba's taverna looked particularly smug.

Then the man from the municipality arrived.

He wasn't rude. Just official. iPad. Sunglasses. The kind of smile that says, "I'm just doing my job," which in Greece usually means, "This is going to ruin your life."

"New regulation," he said, pointing to the tables. "They must be five metres from the shoreline."

Zorba blinked. "They've been here since 1974."

"Yes," the man said. "And now they must move."

To be fair, the rule wasn't completely insane. It was meant to prevent the rise of beach disco bars. Neon-lit monstrosities blaring Europop into the early hours. No one wanted that. But in typical fashion, the law made no exception for charming, slightly slanted tavernas that had been part of village life for generations.

Zorba could have tried to comply, moved the tables inland, served sardines next to the mop bucket. But something in him cracked. Maybe it was the memory of his grandfather, who built the first table with driftwood and rusty nails. Maybe it was the thought of Maria shrilly complaining that the sea "no longer whispered sweet nothings beneath her chair". Maybe it was just that he'd had enough.

He closed the taverna that afternoon. No fanfare. He just turned the chairs upside down, wiped the counter with a sigh, and pulled the shutters down with a final creak that echoed across the beach.

By Wednesday, the village was in shock. By Thursday, it was in mourning.

It was clear that Zorba never made any money from the taverna. But then again, that was never really the point.

The taverna wasn't a business. It was a meeting place. A daily ritual. A local institution that somehow managed to operate without a menu, without receipts, and occasionally without electricity. But that's not what people came for.

They came because this was *their* place. A half-shaded haven where the sea was close enough to smell but far enough to avoid wet feet. Where you could nurse a drink for three hours and nobody would rush you, unless it was to ask if you'd seen their goat. Where arguments flared and fizzled like summer storms, loud, theatrical, and over almost as quickly as they began. Where old women traded gossip with the precision of surgeons, and deals were made with a handshake and an extra glass of *tsipouro*. Where birthday candles were blown out and bottles smashed (sometimes by accident, sometimes not).

Tourists sometimes stumbled in, lured by the hand-painted sign or the promise of "authentic village cooking". They rarely came back. Zorba didn't suffer fools, and he didn't do substitutions. He once chased a German couple down the street with a ladle after they asked if the fish was gluten-free.

But for the regulars, the villagers, the fishermen, the retired schoolteachers, and the man who delivered the bread but stayed until lunchtime, it was sacred ground.

It didn't matter if the floor was cracked, or if the fridge door had to be kicked twice to close. The taverna had heart. It had history. It had that impossible-to-bottle mix of chaos and comfort that only decades of stubborn existence can create.

And now, it was gone. Not because it had failed, but because the rules had changed, and there was no room left for places like this. No line item in the tourism plan for tradition.

When Zorba closed the taverna, no one believed it would last. "He's just sulking," said George. "He'll open again next week."

"He's done this before," Maria added. "Remember when the mayor fined him for serving wine in ketchup bottles? He closed for three days, then reopened with a 'new menu' that was just the same menu but handwritten." He'd also closed once over an argument about parking spaces and once more after a particularly heated debate with the tax inspector involving an expired meat license and a very lively octopus.

But this time was different.

The chairs were stacked for good. The octopus line came down. The fridge hummed to no one. And the place that had been the village's second home, confessional, stage, circus, and parliament, was silent.

At first, people tried to pretend it was temporary. They loitered near the shuttered doors, peering through the slats as if the right angle might reveal a miracle. Yiannis from the post office still sat on the wall across the street with his coffee, staring at it like a retired lighthouse keeper who's lost the sea.

By the end of the first week, the cracks began to show.

With the taverna closed, Dimitri took to drinking his home-made *tsipouro* under the heavy shade of the old fig tree, the same spot where there had once been a crowd of fishermen, loud arguments, and at least one unwary tourist to impress or accidentally poison.

But now he sat alone, cross-legged like a melancholy monk, bottle beside him, glass in hand, recounting old stories to an audience of leaves and lizards. Occasionally, he'd raise his voice as if still arguing with someone about the proper way to cure olives or the superiority of his *tsipouro* to Zorba's, then trail off when he remembered there was no one to contradict him. Every so often he'd take a sip, wince theatrically, then nod with grim satisfaction and mutter, "Good. Still dangerous."

There was something tragic and heroic about it, like a one-man play about defiance, memory, and mild alcohol-induced hallucinations. He'd become his own Greek chorus, answering questions no one asked and occasionally scolding himself for things he may or may not have done in 1997.

The fig tree was a poor substitute for a table full of shouting, laughing, bread-tearing companions. But he stayed there anyway, like a stubborn statue of Dionysus, guarding the last ritual of the village, even if no one else was watching.

Theodora and Mary, ever resourceful in the face of disruption, attempted to relocate their gossip headquarters to the *kafenio*. On paper, it made sense. It had chairs. It had coffee. It had people. But almost immediately, it was clear that the *kafenio* was not a natural habitat for their particular brand of high-frequency village commentary.

For one thing, the atmosphere was all wrong. The place was dominated by old men locked in eternal backgammon tournaments, slapping the dice down with the intensity of a military coup and muttering darkly about each other's grandsons. They weren't exactly the target audience for stories about who had been seen buying hair dye or whose fence was two centimetres taller than it was last year.

Mary gave it a day and a half. By the second morning, she declared that the chair had permanently altered the shape of her spine, the backgammon dice gave her "flashbacks", and worst of all, the whole place reeked of cinnamon. She insisted that the smell was giving her migraines, although there was some debate over whether the cause was the spice, the elderly man who coughed continuously near the sugar packets, or the fact that nobody at the kafenio ever had anything *new* to say.

"It's not natural," she whispered dramatically to her mum. "Everything smells like dessert. Even the ashtrays. And you can only listen to Yiannis explain the fish prices of 1983 so many times before you begin to lose your will to live." She pressed a tissue to her temple like a misunderstood opera singer.

Theodora tried to soldier on. She brought her own cushion one morning. She even tried to inject a little flair into the surroundings by rearranging the condiments and placing a basil sprig in an old yoghurt pot. But by the end of the week, they'd retreated completely, mumbling that it was impossible to carry out any decent surveillance operation without tablecloths, chairs that didn't squeak, and a proper view of the bakery queue.

Zorba's taverna had spoiled them. Where the taverna had been their newsroom, the kafenio was a courtroom with no cases, just ancient men serving life sentences in caffeine and habit.

So Theodora returned to baking, Mary returned to pacing, and both began planning their next move.

Because in this village, if you can't talk about people from your chair, you'll start doing it from your phone. And that, as we all know, is how modern chaos begins.

This was no small thing. Spiros, who treated change the way most people treat food poisoning – rare, unpleasant, and best avoided – had kept the same routine for decades. The only known exception was in 1963, when someone repainted his favourite bench and he refused to sit on the wet paint.

He was a monument more than a man. He claimed to remember the war, though no one could agree which one he meant. He smoked like it was a profession and drank homemade *tsipouro* with the reverence of a priest administering communion. His place at the taverna was sacred. Same bench. Same scowl. Same glass, which he insisted had "aged better than most people".

But with the shutters pulled down and the chairs stacked inside like coffins, Spiros changed.

He started wearing black every day. He stopped shaving, letting his beard bloom into something that looked like it should have its own postcode. His hair, wild and wind-beaten, curled like a laurel wreath for a king no one remembered to crown.

When someone asked him if everything was alright, he waved the question away with a hand that had likely fixed boats, planted olives, and boxed a German in 1945.

"What's there to look nice for?" he grumbled. "The seagulls?"

He took to loitering by the shuttered taverna like a widower waiting outside a locked church; not sad exactly, just… dislocated. Displaced. Like someone who'd lost not a habit, but a home.

Spiros didn't need the food. He didn't even need the company, necessarily. What he needed was the *ritual*. The place to sit, nod once at the world, and drink his *tsipouro* with the silent understanding that life, for all its noise, still had a rhythm – slow, deliberate, and sun-drenched. Without the taverna, that rhythm skipped.

But Spiros was no fool. He was not going to sit in the *kafenio* and listen to men who shuffled cards like they were counting regrets. And he certainly wasn't going to take his drink under a fig tree like Dimitri. That was too much intimacy with nature for his liking.

No: he waited. He scowled at the shutters. He cursed under his breath about "new laws" and "stupid officials" and "that bloody chair", and he held the line. Not just for himself, but for the memory of what the village used to be before it needed permits and politicians to eat grilled sardines by the sea.

Spiros knew the soul of the place had gone quiet. But he also knew something else.

It would speak again.

And when it did, he would be ready. Beard, black clothes and all.

The village felt… off. Like a song with no chorus. Even the sea seemed quieter, as if it was waiting for someone to bring out the chairs and raise a toast to nothing in particular.

As for me, I felt the loss in the small things. In the way Alex stopped walking that little extra loop past the taverna on our evening strolls, pretending she wasn't checking if the chairs had been put out yet, pretending she wasn't hoping for the clatter of plates and the smell of grilled fish on the breeze.

In the silence where the clink of glasses used to rise and fall with the waves, where the smell of charcoal and oregano wrapped the night in a hug warmer than any blanket.

Now it was just shutters. Closed like a mouth that had given up on singing. Five metres had never felt so far.

Five metres. That's all it took. Five metres between the way things were and the way things would now have to be. Five metres between the old stories and the new ones we would somehow, stubbornly, write for ourselves.

Because this is Greece.

And if we're good at anything, it's starting again, with cracked tables, with crooked smiles, with hearts that refuse to close, even when the shutters do.

Chapter Four

Mourning in the Village

By the end of the week, the village looked like someone had drained all the colour from it.

It was one of those afternoons when the heat has softened everything – the sea, the air, and your bones, and even the cicadas sound a little drunk. Alex and I were doing our evening stroll, the one we always did throughout early spring, before the tourists arrived and when the village felt like it still belonged to us.

We paused, as we always did, near the old taverna. The shutters were still closed. The hand-painted sign, crooked but proud, hung stiffly in the stillness. The chairs, once scattered across the patio like old men gossiping, were stacked in mournful silence against the wall.

Alex stared at it for a long time, arms folded, brow furrowed in that way that meant trouble was brewing.

Finally, she said, "It's not right."

I shrugged helplessly.

"Nothing we can do. Zorba made his decision."

Alex was silent for a moment, eyes narrowing slightly – that particular expression she wore whenever she was rearranging reality in her head to suit her plans. Then, without looking at me, she said, "Then we'll just have to make a different decision."

I blinked at her.

"You mean... buy it?"

Alex snorted, shaking her head.

"Buy it? With what? Good wishes and figs? No. Not buy it. Save it."

She turned to me fully, the way a captain turns to their crew right before setting sail into a storm. "We'll take it on. We'll fix it. We'll run it. Not for money. Not for business. For us. For the village."

"For the arguments and the bad wine?" I teased.

"For the life of the village," she said simply.

I looked at the closed shutters again, feeling that ache in my chest, the ache of a home that hadn't quite died, but had gone very quiet.

"And if Zorba says no?" I asked.

Alex shrugged with magnificent Greek indifference.

"Then we pester him until he says yes."

Alex has a particular way of asking for things. What Alex wants, Alex gets. It's never forceful. There's no dramatic persuasion. It's through something far more dangerous: optimism paired with charm. Just a sweet, utterly reasonable suggestion, delivered with such calm certainty that resistance feels not only futile, but impolite.

Like buying land, building a house, even building a Parthenon on our roof.

Now she wanted to reopen Zorba's taverna. What could possibly go wrong?

I asked her, delicately, how she planned to convince him, a man so stubborn he may as well be made of concrete.

Alex shrugged again, with the poised composure of someone who'd already decided how this would end.

"Leave that to me," she replied confidently. "I'll just nag him until he agrees."

It was, in fairness, a strategy that had worked before, most notably when dealing with me, electricians, plumbers, police, and once, memorably, a flock of sheep which arrived to eat our garden with the shepherd who claimed historic grazing rights.

She was already moving, pulling out her phone, tapping furiously, drafting lists and plans and who-knows-what.

Momentum, once Alex found it, was a beautiful and astonishing thing.

I stood there for a moment longer, watching the taverna's broken windows catch the dying sunlight.

It looked battered. Tired. But not beaten. Maybe, just maybe, all it needed was a little stubbornness. A little love.

A little Alex.

As for me, well, I've learned better than to argue with a Greek woman on a mission. Especially when she's carrying the heart of a village in her hands.

***

Which is how, two Sundays later, we found ourselves gathered outside the kafenio, sitting under the fig tree, baking gently in the late afternoon sun, summoned by Alex.

Alex didn't call it a meeting. She called it a *kafeneio conversation*. A casual chat over coffee. Everyone knew better. When Alex wanted to move mountains, she started with coffee.

I sat next to George, who was fidgeting with his *komboloi*, a string of worry beads, like a man about to sit an exam he hadn't studied for. Across from us, Theodora fanned herself with an old, laminated menu, casting the kind of look that could wilt basil, mostly at George, partly at the heat, and partly, I suspected, just for practice.

They didn't speak. They rarely needed to. After forty years of marriage and one formidable daughter, they had perfected the art of marital telepathy, conducted mostly through sighs, shrugs, and the occasional dramatic gesture involving cutlery.

Maria sat nearby, sipping a frappé and eyeing everyone with the alert, predatory stillness of someone who knew three versions of every story and wasn't afraid to tell all of them. Claude had arrived too, all linen and notebook, looking like he might spontaneously burst into poetry at any moment.

Alex stood, hands on hips, surveying the scene. Calm, focused, completely terrifying.

"Well," she said. "We have a choice."

The cicadas buzzed.

"We can sit here and watch the village fade. Watch the tourists drift away. Watch the old men argue in silence and the young ones leave. Or" – here came the pause, the drama, the raised eyebrow of destiny – "we can do something."

Claude leaned forward slightly; notebook already halfway open. George looked for an escape route in the gravel. Dimitri scratched his beard and looked at his bucket, which, yes, still contained a threatening-looking octopus.

"We can reopen the taverna," Alex said, and the words landed like a dropped fork in a quiet room. "Ourselves. Together. A cooperative. No one carrying the full weight. Everyone playing a part."

And that's when it hit me. Between us – this wonderfully mismatched collection of eccentrics, philosophers, bakers, reluctant politicians, goat-wranglers, and people with questionable ideas about seasoning – we actually had everything we needed. Not in the professional sense. In the village sense. The kind of sense where Claude's murals would distract from the wobbly beams, where Maria's obsessive note-taking could double as stock control, and where Theodora could command a kitchen with nothing but a spoon and a glare. We didn't need perfection. We needed each other.

There was a pause. George shifted in his chair. Theodora narrowed her eyes like she was weighing a cut of meat. Maria gasped audibly, already preparing gossip for three different versions of the story. Dimitri blinked, as if trying to work out whether he'd hallucinated the whole thing.

Then Claude leaned forward slowly, like a man at the opera who's just realised it's not a tragedy after all.

Alex clapped her hands once. "Right. Let's talk logistics." Of course, Alex had already thought it through. We weren't about to run a taverna on sheer enthusiasm and fig jam.

"No one's expected to give up their actual lives for this. We're not building a business empire. We're saving the heart of the village, one plate of *moussaka* at a time."

Alex and I were technically retired, or at least that was the dream. We had escaped the stress of city life, shed our credit cards like snakeskin, and arrived in Telios hoping for a quiet life filled with naps, naps that turned into swims, and swims that turned into naps.

Claude lived off a small French pension and claimed he'd moved to the village for the peace and poetry, though one suspected the wine – cheaper than a bottle of water – and the drama had something to do with it.

Dimitri earned his keep by catching fish and fixing things no one else dared to touch. He had no formal schedule, just a mysterious internal compass that always pointed towards *tsipouro* and trouble.

Stamos was a builder in theory, but mostly in the way a cat is a mouse, when it suited him. He helped when he felt like it, especially if someone provided the materials and promised him lunch.

Maria had long since retired, devoting herself full-time to the sacred art of knowing everything before it happened. She considered the taverna her newsroom.

Spiros was older than the vines and just as stubborn. He had been retired so long that most people had forgotten he ever did anything else.

Zorba himself was also retired, or at least he claimed to be, while still showing up each morning to stare at the sea.

Eleni was, technically, retired too, but viewed Greek administration as others view sudoku: a daily challenge to be conquered with stamps, scowls, and surgical precision.

That left Theodora and Mary, who Alex hoped would be our true working force. Unlike the rest of us, they would actually need to be paid. Which was only fair.

Alex had already drawn up a plan for splitting what little profit we expected to make: Mary and Theodora would take a modest wage. The rest of us would work for wine, reputation, and a discount on cheese.

Because this wasn't about making money. It was about keeping something alive.

The village didn't need another business.

It needed a place to be.

"Next, we need roles," Alex said. First, she turned to Theodora. "You are the best cook in the village. Possibly the country. You'll be the chef."

Theodora gave a short, satisfied nod. She was already picturing the menu, and judging us all for our current dietary choices.

Alex continued, "You'll run the kitchen. Full control. That means traditional recipes, no shortcuts, and absolute veto power over any ingredient that looks suspicious or foreign."

"Like parsley in *moussaka*," Theodora muttered, scandalised.

Alex nodded gravely. "Exactly. You are the guardian of flavour. The last defence against menu modernisation."

Theodora beamed, in her own stern, slightly intimidating way.

"Mary," Alex continued, turning to Theodora's daughter, "you are the most beautiful, energetic girl in the village. You'll be the waitress."

Mary adjusted her hair, trying not to smile too much. "I'm not that young any more."

"You're younger than the chairs," Alex said. "You'll be fine."

Mary gave a proud little shrug.

"You'll be the first thing people see," Alex continued. "Warm, welcoming, unstoppable. But also, and this is important, you must enforce order. If someone asks for ketchup with their *souvlaki*, you have full authority to ban them for life."

Mary grinned. "Do I get a whistle?"

"We'll get you one," Alex said.

Together, the Kitchen Queens. "Theodora, Mary, our culinary power duo."

Mary gave a small curtsy. Theodora crossed her arms.

"You'll enforce traditional recipes, reject any talk of fusion cooking, and ruthlessly shame anyone who tries to put feta in the *tzatziki*."

Mary gasped theatrically. "What kind of monster."

"Exactly," Theodora said, already looking for her knife set.

"George," Alex went on, "you'll be in charge of food and beverage acquisition. You'll supply cheese from your workshop and help out with deliveries."

"Done," he said, already calculating how much cheese could fit in the back of his pickup.

"Vassiliki will bake. Bread, *bougatsa*, and whatever those miracle pastries are that you make that reduce grown men to tears. You'll also distract the health inspector with your *koulourakia* if necessary."

Vassiliki nodded solemnly. She was already mentally rearranging her baking schedule.

"Dimitri," Alex said, nodding towards the octopus, "you'll bring the fish."

"Alive?" he asked, uncertain.

"Preferably not," she replied, without missing a beat.

"Stamos!" she shouted, as he wandered by holding a tape measure and what looked suspiciously like a tile cutter. "You'll handle repairs. Only what we ask you to fix."

"No unauthorised walls," I added.

"No promises!" came the reply.

"Claude," Alex continued, "you are in charge of ambience. You'll charm the tourists, pour wine, say complicated French things at sunset. But no jazz nights. We've discussed this."

Claude bowed slightly. His scarf fluttered with unnecessary drama.

"Magnifique," he breathed. "We shall use citronella, candlelight, and a carefully curated playlist."

"No poetry readings," Alex warned.

"Occasionally."

"Absolutely none while food is being served."

He looked devastated.

"And Peter," she said, turning to me with that look, the one I've learned to both fear and adore, "Peter will write. He'll observe everything. He'll document the madness. He'll remember the stories. He'll make sure we don't forget what we fought for."

I raised my glass. "To confusion and cooperation."

The group grumbled in approval. Spiros grunted. A cat appeared from nowhere and jumped on Dimitri's lap. Somewhere in the distance, a rooster crowed, despite it being five o'clock in the afternoon.

Then, from the shade, came Eleni's voice.

"And what about the permits? The five metres? The inspectors with their suspicious moustaches?"

Alex shrugged. Not with defiance, but with the quiet certainty of someone who knew she'd already won. "We'll deal with them... We'll sign their papers. We'll bake them pies. We'll move the tables and smile till they leave. But we will not, *ever*, let them take the soul of this village."

There was a pause.

Then George, with the weariness of a man who knew what came next, said, "If I'm honest... since the taverna closed, I've been eating dinner with my wife every night."

Theodora turned sharply. "And what's wrong with that?"

He raised his hands. "Nothing! Nothing. I just... miss the option."

Laughter broke out. Claude clapped his hands. Even Maria looked momentarily impressed.

Mary leaned in. "If we're doing this, I'll need to know everything. For the uniform design."

"There's a uniform?" I asked.

"There will be," she replied.

Dimitri stood, sloshing a little *tsipouro*. "If there's food, I'm in."

Claude sighed. "I suppose I could design a menu. We can have it in French, with English, German and Greek subtitles."

Eleni muttered, "Fine. But I'm handling the forms. This time, we do it properly."

Alex smiled. A small, knowing smile. The one that said: it's done.

The village had stirred. Not all at once, and certainly not in harmony. But somehow, unmistakably, together.

Chapter Five

Convincing Zorba

Zorba was not a man easily moved.

In fact, he had achieved a level of immovability usually reserved for ancient olive trees and large bureaucratic mistakes.

Once Zorba had made up his mind, about his taverna, about the sea, about the government, about whether or not the octopus was "good today", that was that.

So naturally, Alex decided to change his mind.

"It's simple," she said, marching towards the harbour like a general going into battle. "We explain the plan. We charm him.

We appeal to his sense of tradition."

"And if that doesn't work?" I ask, trying to keep pace.

Alex smiled serenely.

"Then we make him feel really guilty."

It was a solid plan, in that uniquely Greek way where negotiation is fifty percent reasoning, fifty percent volume, and a little bit of divine intervention for good measure.

We found Zorba where he always was these days: by the fisherman's shack, hunched over a battered wooden table, repairing a net that looked like it had seen off more wars than most small countries.

He squinted up at us from under his salt-bleached cap, a cigarette clinging stubbornly to his lower lip.

"Coffee?" Alex offered sweetly, holding up a paper cup like a peace flag.

Zorba grunted, which, in Zorba-language, roughly translated to: *I'll listen, but I'm not promising anything.*

We sat.

Alex launched straight in.

"We want to reopen the taverna," she said.

Zorba blinked at her, as if she'd suggested turning it into a sushi bar.

"Not as a business," she added quickly. "As a community. A cooperative. No one person running it. All of us. Together."

He said nothing, but just kept threading the net with slow, deliberate movements.

I tried to help. "You wouldn't have to do anything, really. We just... need your blessing."

Still nothing.

Alex leaned in closer.

"Zorba," she said, softer now, in that way she had when she was pulling someone's heart out of their chest without them realising it, "this village needs the taverna. We need a place to argue about whether Dimitri actually caught that fish, or just bought it and slapped some seaweed on it for drama. And whether Yiannis's donkey is the ugliest in the region."

A flicker of a smile. Maybe. Or maybe just a twitch.

"You built something real," she said. "We don't need the flashy beach bars or the hotels. We need the taverna. You built that. You gave us a home."

Zorba's hands paused, just for a second, the needle frozen in the tangled mess of twine.

Alex pressed on.

"And now it's our turn to take care of it. To keep it alive."

Zorba stubbed out his cigarette with unnecessary force and stared out at the sea – that endless, familiar horizon where answers usually hid.

"You'll ruin it," he said finally, flat as a fisherman declaring bad weather.

"Probably," Alex agreed cheerfully. "But we'll ruin it with love."

He squinted at us, suspicion battling amusement.

"You'll fight," he said.

"Of course," I said. "It's half the fun."

"You'll argue over the menu."

"Daily," Alex promised.

"You'll run out of fish in the middle of a full house."

"We'll blame Dimitri," I offered.

Zorba shook his head slowly, a reluctant chuckle escaping like a sigh.

"Idiots," he muttered.

"Yes," said Alex. "But we're your idiots."

There was a pause. Long. Heavy. Full of sun and salt and stubbornness.

And then, with the grunt of a man defeated not by argument, but by affection, Zorba leaned back, dug into the pocket of his jacket, and pulled out a rusty old key.

He dropped it into Alex's hand without ceremony.

"You break it," he said, "you fix it."

"And if we fix it?" I asked, hopeful.

He shrugged.

"Then maybe you're not as foolish as you look."

Zorba stood, stretching his back with a crack loud enough to startle a seagull off the nearby railing.

He turned to go, but paused after a few steps, looking back over his shoulder.

"One month," he said. "If you're still open after one month, I'll buy the first round."

"And if we're not?" Alex asked.

Zorba shrugged again, his mouth twitching into something dangerously close to a smile.

"Then at least you tried."

And with that, he turned his back on his net, leaving us sitting there in the warm, heavy evening air, hearts pounding, key in hand, grins wide enough to frighten sensible people.

Conversation over. Blessing given.

Alex squeezed my hand so tightly I thought she might break a finger.

"This," she whispered, her eyes shining with a mixture of madness and hope, "is going to be fun."

And for the first time in weeks, standing there with a rusty key and an impossible dream, I believed her.

CHAPTER SIX

Zorba
The Man, the Myth, the Menu

Zorba was not born in the taverna, though some villagers claimed otherwise. According to legend (and by legend, I mean Maria), his first cry echoed out over the lemon grove and startled three chickens and one sleeping cat. "He came into the world already hungry," she said, "and furious about the olive harvest."

The truth, though simpler, is no less storied. Zorba was born right here in Telios, in the small house behind the church, on a Tuesday so hot the candles melted inside the altar. His father was a fisherman. His mother was the boss. And his education was a family affair: reading and writing courtesy of two older cousins and a very patient aunt, and everything else – life, fish, and how to curse without offending the priest, from his father. From his mother, he learned timing. When to speak, when to stay silent, and exactly how long to stir a pot before the flavour gave up all its secrets. He never forgot any of it. Especially the part about staying silent.

He never set foot in a proper school. But he knew the tides like other children knew their timetables. He could gut a sardine before he could tie his own sandals, and by the time he turned fifteen, he could name every fish in the Aegean and several that had only passed through once.

At eighteen, he was conscripted. National service. With his background and sea legs, the navy made sense. "They gave me a uniform and a kitchen knife," he once said. "One of those was sharp."

He didn't cook fancy food. No sauces with names. No soufflés. Just meals that filled bellies, steadied nerves, and silenced complaints. He learned that onions, if treated with respect, were enough. That lentils had moods. And that even the worst sailor could be won over with a good bean stew and half a loaf of warm bread.

When he returned, he went back to the boat. It was expected. His father was older, the sea was still generous, and fishing was as close to a family inheritance as Telios could offer.

But the joy of cooking had lodged itself somewhere inside him, somewhere beneath the ribs.

So when his grandfather passed away and left behind the old beach taverna, just a few tables, some mismatched chairs, and a charcoal grill that had seen better decades, Zorba didn't hesitate.

He hung up his nets. Picked up a ladle. And stepped behind the counter as though he'd been born there after all.

He never married.

Some say he was too gruff. Others say too gentle. Maria insists he was once in love with a teacher from Chalkida, but she left after one summer, and he never spoke of her again. Maria believes Zorba simply liked his freedom too much – his own company, his own schedule, the right to spend three hours peeling garlic without interruption or small talk.

What's certain is this: he belonged to the village. To all of us. Even if he never said it.

He fed us, fiercely and without fuss: children with scraped knees, tourists with sunburns, locals too tired to cook. You never needed to order. Zorba just looked at you, grumbled something under his breath, and disappeared into the kitchen. Minutes later, something would appear, usually steaming, often slightly charred, occasionally missing a key ingredient, but somehow always exactly what you needed. His food was never fancy. Sometimes not even particularly good. But it tasted like someone had noticed you. And in a world full of menus and noise, that was enough.

He grumbled a lot. About the weather, the fish prices, the rise of plastic chairs. But he never complained about cooking. That, I think, was sacred.

The taverna grew slowly, the way things do here, organically, lopsidedly, without anyone really noticing until it was part of the furniture. Tourists came and sometimes came back. Locals gathered nightly. Arguments started, and were usually settled with olives and another glass of *retsina*.

And Zorba? He stayed behind the grill. Or at the edge of the veranda. Always watching, never centre stage. He didn't want applause. Just empty plates and a comfortable silence where there had once been hunger.

He aged but never slowed. The moustache grew longer, the opinions sharper, but his hands remained steady, and his food kept coming.

He rarely told stories about the past. But once, during a late night with too much wine and only a sliver of moon, I asked him what made him happiest.

He thought for a long time.

Finally, he said, "When someone eats, and then leans back, and says nothing. That's the moment. Right after the food, right before the praise. The silence. That's mine." He looked at his glass, shrugged, and added, "Also, good sardines."

That was Zorba. Cook. Sailor. Philosopher in disguise. The man who fed the village for decades, and asked nothing but an honest appetite in return.

And when people say, "He never married," I always think: he didn't need to.

He married the sea. The taverna. The olive trees.

He married the village.

And all of us, whether we knew it or not, were part of the family.

CHAPTER SEVEN

Partners in Crime (and *Tsipouro*)

Organising a cooperative in Greece is like herding cats. Drunk, sunburned, and related. They'll argue, wander off, stop for a snack, and then, just when you're ready to give up, everything falls perfectly into place.

We called a meeting on the old patio of Zorba's taverna. No agenda. No minutes. No chance of sticking to the topic for more than five minutes at a time. Just a long table, a few wobbling chairs, and enough coffee and ouzo to fuel a small revolution.

Zorba came, of course.

He sat slightly apart, arms folded, wearing the permanent scowl of a man who wasn't officially involved, but was absolutely judging every decision.

Alex opened proceedings with a smile that could have launched a thousand ships, or at least a small fishing fleet.

"We're not here to make money," she said. "We're here to keep the taverna alive. Everyone has a part to play. No deadweight; everyone will pull together to make it work."

There was a general murmur of agreement. The kind of murmur that suggests most people hadn't fully listened but trusted there'd be food involved eventually.

"Most of you already know your roles. But I've done some more thinking. Firstly, Zorba," she said, "you remain our fearless leader and owner. In name, if not in motion." Zorba looked up from his coffee, squinted, and nodded once.

"Duties include general advice, drinking coffee, shaking your head when we mess something up, and reminding us that we're doing it wrong, with feeling."

"Authority respected selectively," I added helpfully.

Zorba grunted. It sounded like approval. Or possibly indigestion.

"And I," she continued, "will handle menus, suppliers, bookings, and staff revolts. No one needs to call me boss."

"Because we'll already know," Maria muttered, scribbling in her own suspiciously glittery notebook.

"Maria, congratulations," Alex said. "You are now in charge of PR."

Maria lit up. "So I get to make announcements?"

"No. You get to make announcements that are only about 60 per cent true."

"That's most of them already," she said brightly.

"And please," I added, "no more leaking 'celebrity' sightings to the press."

"It was one time," she said. "And that actor really did *look* like Tom Hanks."

"He was Scottish."

"And short."

"And twelve."

Maria shrugged. "Details."

"And of course, Father Evangelos."

The priest raised his coffee cup in blessing.

"You will bless the kitchen, the tables, our effort, and perhaps the fridge, if it misbehaves again."

"And the wine?" he asked.

"If you must."

"Finally," Alex said, turning to Eleni, who was already clicking her pen with the menace of a woman ready for war. "Eleni, you are our administrator."

Eleni smiled like a wolf. "I've already filed two forms you didn't ask for and one complaint about the chair permits."

"Perfect," Alex said. "Your duties include navigating paperwork, regulations, and anything written in uppercase Greek with a stamp in the corner."

"And arguing with inspectors," I added.

"And winning," she finished.

At some point, inevitably, we had to name the thing. Which is to say, Alex made coffee, Maria brought unsolicited opinions, Claude suggested five alternative branding concepts, and I suggested, quite reasonably, that we call it *The Parthenon by the Sea*.

It had a ring to it. It connected the dots. Besides, it was poetic. It had metaphorical weight.

Which is precisely why everyone ignored me.

"The Parthenon?" Maria asked, eyebrows climbing into her fringe. "Is it a taverna or a museum?"

"It's pretentious," said Dimitri, though he pronounced it *pre-tensious*, which didn't help his case.

Claude offered a monologue about brand continuity and emotional resonance, but Alex cut him off with a wave.

"No," she said. "We're not naming it after an ancient ruin. We're bringing something back to life."

And just like that, it was decided.

Zorba's.

Simple. Honest. Familiar. The name that had hung above the patio for fifty years, faded by salt and sun but never forgotten.

I may have been overruled, but just between us, I'm still calling it *The Parthenon by the Sea* as a subtitle. Artistic licence.

One of the few perks of being the one holding the pen.

"So," Alex said, clapping her notebook shut. "That's it. Those are the roles. Together, we will run this taverna. No one carries it alone."

Zorba raised his glass in salute. Mary popped open her lipstick. Dimitri produced a fish. And I, for my part, quietly made a note in the back of my own little book: "Madness. Organised. Sort of."

And that, I think, was a very good beginning.

***

Eleni attacked paperwork with the same intensity most people reserve for football finals.

If there was a stamp to be found, a signature to be bullied out of a trembling civil servant, Eleni would find it. When she joined the cooperative, we all slept a little better. The local tax office, however, probably had emergency meetings about her.

If Greece has a national sport, it isn't football. It's paperwork. Specifically, producing enough forms to rebuild the Acropolis twice over, then demanding them again, this time with blue stamps, three witnesses, and a goat to verify authenticity.

Opening a taverna, even one that had already been open since the days when electricity was just a rumour, meant forms. Licenses. Permissions. Health certificates. Fire inspections. Special permits for serving alcohol within five metres of a tree. (Yes. Really.)

Alex, naturally, was undaunted.

"How bad can it be?" she said, sharpening her pencil like a weapon of hope.

Very bad, as it turned out.

Eleni arrived at our kitchen like she meant business: black coffee in one hand, a battered leather folder in the other, and the sort of expression that could curdle yoghurt.

"We need," she announced, slapping the folder onto the table with enough force to rattle the cutlery, "a hygiene certificate, a business license, a coastal use permit, a fire-safety inspection, proof that our kitchen staff have completed food handling courses, a certified map showing the tables exactly five metres, no less, from the shoreline" – she paused – "and, a certificate from the archaeological department confirming that we are *not*, in fact, operating over the ruins of an ancient temple."

I looked at Alex.

Alex looked at me.

We both looked at the ceiling, hoping for divine intervention.

Naturally, the village had its own ideas about handling paperwork.

Dimitri offered to "borrow" some certificates from his cousin's abandoned restaurant two villages over.

Claude suggested creating "artistic interpretations" of permits, painted in watercolours.

Vassiliki proposed solving everything the traditional way: with a tray of her lethal baklava.

Maria, meanwhile, had already spread word that all permits were secured and that Gordon Ramsay might be attending the opening.

Meanwhile, Spiros muttered darkly about the last time the government came to inspect in 1982, three *tsipouros* deep, when the inspector fell off his chair and declared the kitchen "perfectly compliant, more or less".

Nothing about this process was quick. Or logical. Or, frankly, legal.

At one point, Eleni had to prove that our toilets were accessible *but not so accessible* that they attracted "non-customer wandering". Claude suggested building a philosophical labyrinth to the bathroom. He was gently but firmly overruled.

In the end, it wasn't logic that won. It was the baklava.

The mayor's secretary, the human bottleneck of our permits, had a well-documented weakness for Vassiliki's walnut-stuffed, honey-dripping baklava.

Vassiliki baked. We delivered. The next morning, half the required stamps appeared as if by magic. We didn't ask too many questions. In Greece, when a door opens, you don't argue about who unlocked it. You walk through it quickly, and you bring coffee.

But we weren't finished yet. Not even close. There were still forms missing, tables to measure, and an angry call from the coastal inspector accusing our tin roof of "leaning in a suspicious manner".

But for the first time, the dream of reopening Zorba's taverna didn't feel impossible any more.

It felt messy. Chaotic. Full of argument, laughter, and unexpected kindness. In other words: exactly right.

Chapter Eight

Building the Dream
(and Other Poor Decisions)

Once the paperwork had been applied for, the forms had been filled, and some stamps had been obtained, we needed to wait for official permission, which could take some time. Nobody had said no yet, so we took that as a licence to carry on. It was time to tackle the next great challenge: fixing the taverna.

In theory, this meant minor repairs. A lick of paint here. A new chair leg there. Maybe even a functioning fridge, if we dared to dream. In practice, this meant handing the entire project over to Stamos and Dimitri. Which was, in retrospect, about as sensible as asking two donkeys to renovate a library.

Stamos arrived on the first morning with a cigarette behind his ear, a bent tape measure, and the air of a man who had no intention of following any building codes written this century. Dimitri followed behind him carrying a crate of suspiciously rusted tools, two sea urchins, and what appeared to be a toilet seat.

"Preparation is everything," Stamos said, dropping his hammer with a dramatic flourish. It bounced off the floor and narrowly missed Claude's foot.

I looked at Alex. She looked at me. We both looked at the sky again, which by this point had stopped offering answers. According to Stamos, the following were "essential improvements":

- Rebuilding the lean-to tin roof "properly", meaning taller, wider, and, ideally, capable of hosting a medium-sized wedding without prior notice. It would dramatically transform into a pergola.
- Installing a pizza oven "because everyone likes pizza". (No one had requested pizza.)
- Adding a third entrance "for good luck".

According to Dimitri, the following were also "necessary":

- A fish tank made from an old bathtub.
- A wooden deck "for sunset dancing".
- A secret storeroom for "special catches" (no further details provided).

Claude, meanwhile, suggested installing mood lighting and a sculpture garden.

He was politely ignored.

By mid-morning, the taverna looked less like a place of business and more like the aftermath of a small and confused tornado. The pergola beams arrived, all two metres too long. The fridge was discovered to be leaking. The plumbing under the sink was held together with something that looked suspiciously like dental floss.

Spiros sat on his usual bench, shaking his head slowly and muttering *"Olokliri katastrofi"* (complete disaster) into his *tsipouro*.

Maria, of course, had already begun reporting live updates from the scene to anyone within earshot: "The pergola is falling over." "They're using sea urchins to fix the wiring." "Claude wants to put up a French flag in the kitchen!" Only half of these things were technically true.

After the third time a beam fell over (narrowly missing Vassiliki, who responded by swearing in three languages and throwing a rolling pin), Alex had had enough.

She marched into the bedlam, hands on hips, voice sharp enough to cut timber.

"Stamos! Pergola first. No pizza oven. Dimitri! No bathtub. Claude! No existential lighting until we have a working toilet!"

Everyone froze. Even the seagulls seemed to pause mid-flight.

Alex pointed at the battered chalkboard sign still leaning against the old wall.

"This taverna," she said, "is not a resort. It's not a disco. It's not a museum. It's a place where people come to sit, eat, drink, argue, and live. Simple. Honest. Greek."

There was a beat of silence. Then George, emerging from behind a dangerously leaning wall, said quietly, "I'll get the nails."

Spiros grunted approvingly.

And just like that, the chaos, while not exactly *reduced*, became more purposeful.

Over the next few days:

The pergola was built. It had columns like the Parthenon, so I was happy. It was slightly crooked, but charming.

The tables were sanded and painted.

The chairs were patched up with rope, nails, and optimism.

The fridge was coaxed back into life (mostly).

The smell of lemon oil, old wood, fresh coffee, and hope filled the air.

The bar, which was technically a plank across two oil drums, was polished.

It wasn't perfect. But then again, neither was the real Parthenon. And that had lasted a few thousand years, give or take a cannonball or two, and an avaricious English lord (best not talk about that).

By the end of the week, battered, bruised, and covered in splinters, we stood back and looked at what we had built. A little wobbly. A little wild. But completely, gloriously alive.

Our Parthenon by the Sea was nearly ready.

All we had to do now… was open the doors. And pray the kitchen tap didn't explode first.

CHAPTER NINE

LEMONS, WINE, AND OTHER DISASTERS

Zorba's taverna had forever sat close to the sea, hugging the curve of the coast like it knew how to listen. Its little front courtyard, just big enough for four tables and one suspicious cat, sat beneath a corrugated tin roof that creaked in the sun and roared in the rain. In the winter, the wind turned it into a percussion instrument. Every northerly gust sent a fresh chorus of rattles through the metal sheets and shook the plastic windbreakers until they flapped like sails in a storm.

On quiet afternoons, if you listened carefully, you could hear the arguments inside. On stormy days, you could only assume they were still happening.

Most of the tables had always been scattered across the beach, set out like driftwood offerings to the gods. A few balanced under the old eucalyptus tree, others just leaned into the shingle as best they could. Now, the new Five-Metre Rule complicated things, of course. The sea didn't exactly respect measuring tape, and neither did the locals.

But Spiros's bench couldn't move. That was non-negotiable.

It sat beneath a knotted olive tree with one root that looked suspiciously like a goat's horn, and no one remembered a time it hadn't been there. Not even Spiros. He simply adjusted his cushion depending on the season and nodded once each morning to the sea. It wasn't tradition. It was law.

Fortunately, if the tide was out and there was an offshore wind, the bench was just about legal. At least five metres from the sea, more or less. It would be easier to argue with the inspector than with Spiros.

So we measured, adjusted, rearranged, and with some creative spacing (and Spiros's silent blessing), we managed eleven tables and one immovable bench. Seven on the beach, and four under the pergola; not ideal, but workable.

But our taverna dreams were outpacing our floor plan. The tables were too close, the patio too narrow, and we were one seating arrangement away from putting chairs in the middle of the road. Not unheard of in Greece, but not ideal when the mayor's cousin is the traffic officer and takes a dim view of al fresco dining on a public thoroughfare. We had thought about putting a table or two on a floating pontoon – the law didn't actually forbid tables in the sea – but Mary would need a snorkel to deliver the drinks, and there was always a risk our clients may float off towards Skiathos if the wind was in the wrong direction.

We stood at the edge of the patio one afternoon, surveying the tables. Claude was arguing with himself about optimal lantern placement, waving a scarf in one hand and a lightbulb in the other like a conflicted interior designer in crisis. Stamos was gesturing skyward with a plank of wood, muttering about a second deck level. "We just need scaffolding and faith," he said, as if this were a perfectly normal structural plan.

Alex, who had been quietly observing the confusion with that dangerous look of creative calculation, tilted her head towards the rusting chain-link fence beside the taverna.

"What about that?" she asked.

That was the lemon grove.

At first glance, it looked like nothing. A tangle of forgotten greenery trying its best to recall better days. A stubborn patch of lemon trees, thirty of them, gnarled and glorious, still scattered sunlight like confetti and dropped fruit with theatrical indifference. Wild oregano crept beneath them, competing for attention with ancient weeds and more bees than one should reasonably allow.

The gate sagged from a single hinge like it had given up sometime in the eighties, and a fig tree had made a confident claim on the back corner.

But if you paused, tilted your head slightly and squinted, you could see it.

The grove stretched just far enough to fit ten or fifteen tables. There was a flat space near the front, perfect for Spiros's emergency bench, The far-left corner held the skeleton of a herb garden, still defiantly sprouting thyme. A few vacant beehives leaned under a low hedge forming the far boundary.

There was a patch of earth near the fig tree, firm enough to host a hammock or two if one got ambitious about relaxation. Children played there occasionally. Dimitri had once been spotted retrieving what may have been a fishing net or a former relative. No one ever claimed ownership of it. But no one had denied it either.

It was public in the way things become public in Greece: through time, use, and a general shrug of collective assumption.

Just maybe, this could solve our problem.

So, like all great schemes in the village, this one began with a lack of space and an abundance of ideas.

We had chairs. We had tables. We even had Claude's deeply questionable attempt at bunting: three metres of frayed ribbon tied between two bamboo poles and described, with great enthusiasm, as "rustic". But what we didn't have was space. Not for the musicians, the stray tourists, the extended family members of extended family members, or the inevitable goat someone would absolutely bring along without asking.

So we turned to the grove. And that's when things started to get interesting.

Alex ran her fingers through the leaves like a mother checking for fever. "We could string lights. Maybe hang a hammock."

I nodded, cautiously. "Do we actually… own this?" I asked aloud. "Perhaps it comes with the taverna, and everyone forgot about it."

There was silence. The kind of silence that suggests paperwork is not involved.

That evening, we found Zorba outside the taverna, sipping his coffee like it had betrayed him personally.

"Zorba," Alex said, as the light curled golden over the patio, "the grove. Behind the taverna. Do you know who owns it?"

She said it casually, but it wasn't casual.

Zorba didn't answer at first. He didn't even blink. He just sat there, staring out to sea, the same way he had done every day for as long as anyone could remember – as if waiting for an answer to arrive with the tide.

When he finally spoke, it was more to the horizon than to us.

"Might be mine," he said. "Or my uncle's. Or the church's. Depends on who's asking."

There was a pause. A quiet one. The kind that settles when something delicate is being held.

"We're asking," I said, softly.

He turned, finally looking at us. Not unkindly. Just… measured.

"Then it's probably mine," he said. And then he added, after a beat, "There might be a deed. Somewhere."

He didn't offer to find it. He didn't need to. The words were enough, a gate unlocked, just a little.

That "somewhere" turned out to be a rusting biscuit tin wedged in the back of a drawer in the storage room. A drawer that hadn't been opened in years, possibly decades. It was buried beneath broken fishing reels, faded ID cards, and a stack of government forms yellowed to the colour of old cheese and stamped with dates from the nineteen seventies.

We opened it slowly, reverently. Like archaeologists excavating a tomb of forgotten kings.

Inside, nestled between a receipt for nails and a photograph of a man with a moustache, was a single sheet of paper. Faded, curled at the edges. But still legible.

"*To Chorafi me Lemonies.*" The Lemon Grove.

We brought it to Zorba.

He took it without speaking, held it in his hands like something heavier than it looked. He squinted at the handwriting as if it belonged to a ghost. When he finally spoke, it wasn't with his usual grumble.

"If you're all going to care for it," he said quietly, "then use it. Keep it alive. Just don't let it go wild again."

He stood slowly, the paper still in his hand. Then, turning to go, he added, almost as an afterthought, but not really, "Just don't let it forget who it belongs to."

And that was the moment. The moment the grove stopped being forgotten, and started remembering. The moment the lemon grove went from abandoned wasteland to disputed paradise. From silence to spectacle. Because once the grove had a name, and a use, it also had suitors.

Outside, someone shouted about tomatoes. A moped backfired. The sea kept breathing.

We planned, of course, to say nothing. Not until we knew more. But this was a Greek village.

By sunrise, Maria had already told four people we'd found a treasure map. By midday, someone had suggested the grove was cursed. By evening, Eleni was drawing up business plans for a Lemon and Olive Women's Cooperative, and Dimitri was testing how lemon peels reacted when steeped in his strongest spirit. ("It glows," he said. "That's normal.")

No one had ever asked if we owned the lemon grove. They just asked what we'd do with it.

And Zorba?

He knew, of course. He always knew. That patch of land had belonged to his uncle, then had quietly been passed down, unspoken but understood. It had never been farmed commercially, never sold, never measured for profit, just left to the bees and the wind.

Zorba wandered past while we were waist-deep in brambles and lemon thorns, Alex muttering to herself and Dimitri brandishing a rake like he was facing down a wild boar.

He paused at the edge of the fence and leaned on his stick. He said nothing for a long time.

Then, slowly, he stepped through the open gate, like it was still his, but also… no longer quiet.

He reached up, picked a lemon, held it to his nose, and gave a small nod.

We never knew if he meant to offer us the grove, or just the chance to keep it alive – the place, the people, the memory.

Not ownership. Not exactly. Just trust, wrapped in silence and lemon trees.

Either way, we took it as a blessing.

***

The lemon grove, until now, had been a kind of secret garden. Wild. Uneven. Overflowing with branches and bees and the scent of something that might be either bliss or hay fever. It came with no instructions, a broken fence, and one deeply suspicious tortoise who'd claimed the northern corner as his personal kingdom.

Alex saw potential. I saw nettles. Her plan, as always, was simple on paper: tidy the grove, clear the undergrowth, prune the trees, and make space for paths. Then invite the villagers in.

The lemon trees stayed, of course – they were the heart of the place. We would just coax them out of tangles and give them room to breathe.

Reality, of course, had other ideas.

We began with the clearing. Dimitri arrived with a chainsaw, and a plan that involved "encouraging biodiversity through selective pruning". Claude showed up in linen, pronounced it "a living metaphor", and wandered off to sketch trees.

We found old irrigation lines. Bits of pottery. A rusted bicycle. And, unnervingly, what might have been part of a government sign from 1973.

"I think we need permission," I said, already feeling the paperwork itch behind my eyes.

Alex waved me off. "We'll do it properly. Eleni's on it."

Eleni, of course, was thrilled. Not by the grove, which she referred to as "an administrative hazard with foliage", but by the challenge. She launched into it like a general, filing forms, making calls, and muttering darkly about agricultural zoning codes written by lunatics with a fear of citrus.

The list of requirements was even more baffling than the ones to open the taverna. To use the grove, we needed a community use permit, a safety certificate, a botanical impact assessment, a fire-prevention strategy, and, inexplicably, a certified map proving we weren't in a migratory sheep corridor.

A week later, Eleni arrived clutching a plastic folder and a facial expression that suggested she'd either just won a minor legal battle or lost one and decided not to care.

"These are for you," she said, dropping the folder onto the table. It made a noise like unfinished business.

Inside: twenty-seven forms, two official stamps, and one very unofficial bribe in the form of a lemon cake.

We signed everything. Twice. Sometimes in red.

Claude witnessed it with a solemn nod and a glass of wine.

"It's done," Eleni said. "Or at least, it's happening. Possibly illegally. But it's Greece, so that's practically the same thing."

While Eleni battled the civil service, the village took sides. Maria immediately began spreading rumours that we were turning the grove into a nudist colony or a luxury resort. Possibly both. Theodora was deeply concerned that people would trample her herbs. George wanted to know if he could sell cheese there. Zorba just grunted and asked if we'd be serving wine.

Alex, undeterred, kept going. She gathered everyone together under the olive tree, drew plans in the sand. Mary designed signs. Vassiliki baked lemon pies "for inspiration".

Stamos installed a swing no one asked for. Claude hosted a sunset reading to a confused but polite Slovenian tourist who was just looking for the loo.

We cut back branches. We levelled the ground. We painted stones white and called them borders. We even planted lavender, though the tortoise objected strongly and tried to eat it. But slowly, it worked. The grove began to take shape.

But, before we could finalise our plans for the grove, we had a taverna to open. We would work with what we had; the grove could wait a little longer.

CHAPTER TEN

THE (NOT SO) SOFT OPENING

While lemon grove madness quietly fermented in the background, Dimitri decided that the taverna's reopening needed a "house spirit".

He proudly produced three large bottles of his home-made *tsipouro*: clear, potent, and smelling faintly of nail-varnish remover.

Tsipouro, for the uninitiated, is a clear grape-based spirit that tastes like burning and feels like truth. It is poured at weddings, baptisms, funerals, and arguments. It is *not* for the faint of heart, the weak of liver, or the overly self-aware.

Claude insisted on a tasting.

After one sip, he staggered backwards, clutching his throat like a tragic French opera singer, proclaiming he had "seen death, and it wore flip-flops".

Maria took a shot, declared temporary blindness, and threatened to sue Dimitri for damages and emotional distress.

Father Evangelos, ever gracious, blessed the bottle with a murmured prayer and promptly tipped his glass into a potted basil plant when no one was looking. The basil turned brown within the hour.

Alex, with the same steely authority she once used to negotiate with a Greek electricity company, banned Dimitri's *tsipouro* from the premises with immediate effect. Dimitri sulked, audibly and with dramatic sighs. He announced, to no one in particular, that he would drink the entire batch himself, out of sheer principle and mild spite. But he stopped short of pouring another glass, muttering that he was going fishing in the morning, and temporary blindness wasn't ideal for aiming a trident.

Claude decided this was the perfect time to "elevate" the wine selection.

He sourced three barrels of "authentic village wine" from the butcher's cousin. No one remembered seeing wine in actual wooden barrels for years. Most of it until now had come in second-hand plastic water bottles. These were so rustic it made our taverna look like The Ritz.

"Organic! Romantic!" Claude declared, tapping one barrel

proudly. The barrel immediately cracked. A high-pressure geyser of pink wine shot across the taverna patio, baptising Stamos, a passing cat, and two innocent beach chairs. Claude, dripping and delighted, called it "a sign of blessing". Stamos, less poetically, called it "a bloody disaster" and went home to find dry trousers.

By the day before opening, the combination of the Exploding Wine Incident, the mysteriously powerful *tsipouro*, and the general pre-launch hysteria had turned the village into something resembling a very theatrical dress rehearsal, just without a script, a director, or any agreement on what the play was about.

Vassiliki flatly refused to bake anything further until "someone dealt with the kitchen's strange atmosphere", which she claimed was making the dough nervous. Maria suggested we bring in both the priest *and* a lifestyle coach to restore balance. Eleni demanded a fully documented Cooperative Constitution, complete with bylaws, emergency amendments, and a section on seating rights during high season.

Claude set up folding chairs and tealights under the pergola and began referring to it as a "zone of spiritual readiness".

Dimitri began assembling a bonfire out of old pallets, explaining that it was "precautionary" and might double as a seafood smoker, depending on the wind.

Alex, on the other hand, remained calm.

Not the quiet kind of calm, the dangerous kind. The kind she gets right before a major idea, or a spontaneous furniture rearrangement.

Her hair was tied up. Her eyes narrowed in that particular way that said: *I have a plan. And I'm really hoping none of you ruin it.*

She moved through the mayhem like a general directing a battalion of very drunk cats – steady, silent, and not above using a tea towel as a signalling device.

By the time we'd noticed, she'd already restored some kind of order.

Not normal order.

Alex-order.

Which is far more efficient, slightly alarming, and somehow involves string.

"We are opening," she said, standing in the middle of the dusty patio. "If the sky falls, if the lemons fall, if Dimitri starts levitating, we are still opening."

And somehow, despite everything, I believed her.

That night, the taverna stood ready. For the most part. The pergola leaned slightly to the left. The chairs creaked when you breathed near them. The tables were slowly sinking into the sand. The new hand-painted sign had a spelling mistake we chose to ignore. The lemon grove rustled softly behind us, a half-forgotten promise of future disorder. And in the air, thick with the smell of thyme, salt, and impending disaster, was something else: hope.

And Spiros? That evening, without fuss or announcement, he reappeared freshly shaved, the beard gone, the hair tamed.

He claimed it was "for hygiene", but we all knew it meant something else. Zorba's was opening. The village was stirring. And the king, apparently, had crowned himself.

Tomorrow, we would open the doors. Come what may.

* * *

Soft launch. Such a lovely phrase. It conjures up images of polite crowds, gentle applause, a few minor hiccups easily smoothed over with a smile and a complimentary ouzo.

What it *doesn't* conjure up is: a kitchen fire caused by Claude trying to flambé the salad, Dimitri offering *tsipouro* shots to underage tourists, Maria live-reporting every disaster to the entire village via the bakery window, and, just before dusk, a goat wandering onto the patio.

Not *a* goat in the abstract village-goats-wandering-the-roads sense. *This* goat was personal.

White with a splash of grey, eyes full of mischief, and a little bell that clinked. She arrived without invitation, trotting confidently up the beach path as if summoned by divine mandate. She paused at the taverna entrance, sniffed the air, and walked in like she owned it.

She chewed a napkin. She nibbled the corner of a cushion. Then she calmly climbed onto a low stool and laid down.

"Whose goat is that?" I asked. "She's not mine," said George. "She's not mine either," said Yiannis the postman, watching helplessly as she delicately sampled the printed menu, then moved on to the bowl of communal olives with the air of a food critic.

Claude was enchanted. "She has presence," he whispered. "Mystery."

Alex crossed her arms. "She's eating the menu."

And just like that, Katerina the Goat joined the cast.

The sun dropped behind the hills in a smudge of pink and gold, and the sea turned the colour of old silver.

Dimitri arrived in a cloud of fish smell, balancing a crate of seafood of uncertain origin on one shoulder, and a bottle of "improved" *tsipouro* in the other.

Alex stood by the door, clipboard in one hand, a slight sheen of sweat on her brow, looking every inch the battle commander about to storm Normandy. I adjusted a few chairs. Claude adjusted a candle. Dimitri adjusted his expectations.

The first guests began to trickle in. Curious locals, slightly nervous tourists, distant cousins and a German couple who were definitely reviewing us live online. But it didn't take long for the first cracks to appear.

The fridge gave up with a gentle sigh and a faint electrical burning smell. The grill worked, provided you stood at a 45-degree angle and swore loudly in Greek. The pergola, under the collective weight of Claude's fairy lights and Dimitri's "lucky fishing net", began to sag just enough to alarm anyone over six feet tall. Meanwhile, the tables, lovingly sanded, nailed, and blessed, wobbled like drunken flamingos as the tablecloths tried to escape even after Stamos had nailed them to the tables.

Maria took one look at the seating arrangements and announced loudly to no one in particular, "If the tables collapse, it's because the lemon grove is cursed."

It was about an hour in, just as things were beginning to settle, wine flowing, *saganaki* sizzling, laughter rising, when Katerina the goat made her move.

With the timing of a professional comedian, she strutted onto the patio, dragging someone's laundry behind her like a cape. She paused by a tourist's plate, sniffed, and delicately consumed another paper napkin. Claude tried to recite something French. She headbutted his shin and moved on. Maria, barely containing herself, narrated the event live to the bakery.

Yiannis arrived with a rope and a baguette, declaring himself on "goat extraction duty".

Alex, broom in hand, quietly removed the goat from the dining area, eyes blazing. Katerina returned ten minutes later through the lemon grove. No one questioned it.

And yet... despite the broken fridge, the sagging pergola, the goat invasion, the fact that we ran out of bread halfway through the evening (Dimitri blamed the lemon grove, obviously), despite all of it, something extraordinary happened.

People stayed. They laughed. They ate the saganaki with their fingers when the cutlery ran out. They toasted each other with slightly warm wine. They argued about football and politics and whose grandmother made the best *kleftiko*. For the first time in months, the village felt alive again.

Not perfect, never perfect. But real. Messy. Loud. Full of terrible singing and too many hugs and a sense of stubborn, stupid, wonderful hope.

Alex looked around at the chaos, at George balancing a broken chair with a wine bottle, at Dimitri teaching two Norwegian backpackers how to drink *tsipouro* properly (badly), at Maria whispering into her phone with the glee of a reporter covering the end of the world, and she smiled. A slow, deep, satisfied smile. We had done it. Somehow, against every logical prediction, we had done it.

Zorba's taverna, The Parthenon by the Sea, had reopened.

And in that moment, with the lemon grove rustling quietly behind us and the stars coming out one by one over the cracked roof and crooked tables, it didn't matter that the menu was misspelled, or that Claude's lights flickered like a haunted disco. It mattered that we were here. Together. Alive. A little drunk. And gloriously, imperfectly, completely Greek.

There was just one small problem. We still weren't allowed to open. Not officially. Not legally. Not in any way that involved accepting actual money in exchange for actual food.

Due to a minefield of permits, forms, counter-forms, contradictory advice from the municipality, and one handwritten note from a man called Nikos who may or may not have been the coastal inspector, we were still awaiting "final approval". From *someone*. Possibly several departments. No one could say for sure.

Until we got all the many mysterious forms and inspections under our belt, with the right rubber stamps applied in the correct order on the appropriate colour-coded forms, technically, we weren't open. Not officially. We didn't have the full permission yet – just a hopeful nod from Eleni and a promise that the paperwork was "in progress" (which in Greece means anywhere between three days and the next Olympics). So, we called it a "soft launch". No menu. No receipts. No prices. Guests wandered in, found a seat, and were handed food and wine with no mention of money. They left what they could. Or what they thought it was worth. One man left a poem. Someone else donated a jar of anchovies. Claude started a tab system on the back of a paper napkin. Technically, we were just "testing the layout". Legally? Let's say it was a dinner party with 23 friends we hadn't met yet.

"It won't take long," Eleni assured us, waving a folder the thickness of a taverna menu and written entirely in capital Greek acronyms. "Just a few more signatures, one coastal adjustment form, and the fire chief's second cousin's approval."

So we waited.

INTERLUDE

PART 1

ON LOVE AND ALEX

There are two things you should know before we go any further.

The first is that nothing – *nothing* – prepares you for Greek love.

It's loud. It's stubborn. It involves far too much food and the occasional threat of divine punishment. It's the kind of love that doesn't whisper, it *declares*. That interrupts your thoughts to tell you to wear a scarf because there's a breeze and death is always potentially just one draught away. It's not romantic in the traditional sense, but it is fierce, and funny, and completely uninterested in subtlety.

And the second thing you should know is that I fell in love with Alex precisely because of all of that.

We didn't meet on a sunlit Greek island over a plate of sardines or during some windswept ferry drama involving feta cheese and bureaucracy. That would've made a good story, but the real one's better.

We met in England. Teenagers. Half-formed. Both slightly out of place.

She was Greek, with eyes that saw more than she let on, and the kind of laugh that made everything else around it feel less serious.

I was English. Predictable. Thoughtful. Possibly wearing a cardigan.

We lost touch, as people do. Life swept in. Years passed. Countries changed. But something lingered.

And then, two decades later, by sheer accident or cosmic mischief, we met again.

No planning. No expectation.

Just... there she was.

The same laugh. The same fire. A quiet certainty that somehow, this was always meant to be.

And from that moment, everything changed.

She pulled me – joyfully, gently – into a life I didn't know

I'd been waiting for.

A life full of noise, food, family, beauty, hatred of the government, goats, love, and lemon trees.

Alex is… how can I put this… Greek in all the best ways.

Passionate. Proud. Stubborn as an old olive tree and just as deeply rooted. She has the eyes of a philosopher and the temper of a well-aimed frying pan.

I was English, once. I wore socks with sandals, said sorry when someone else bumped into me, and thought dinner after 8 p.m. was outrageous. But after Alex, I didn't stand a chance.

She drew me into a world of ouzo-soaked mayhem, late-night politics, and family lunches that lasted until dinner. I was seduced by her smile, disarmed by her sense of justice, and hopelessly undone by the way she could turn a ruined shopping list into a love letter. And so I followed her.

From London to Athens. From Athens to Telios. Moving to Athens was like stepping into a whirlpool, specifically one fuelled by home-made wine and conflicting family advice.

And yet, I adored it. Even when I didn't understand it. Even when I didn't understand *her*.

Alex would translate the words, but it was her presence that made the culture make sense. When I floundered at bureaucratic counters, she stood beside me like a storm. When I got lost in the town and ended up in someone's kitchen (long story), she laughed first, then helped me apologise with a bottle of wine.

She taught me how to shout affectionately. How to argue

without malice. How to forgive in the time it takes to pass the bread.

And, eventually, she taught me how to live in Greece.

When we arrived in Telios, I thought we were coming for peace. A slower life. Fewer arguments. No more 4 a.m. ferry queues. What I didn't understand then, but what she did, is that peace doesn't mean silence. It means knowing your place in the noise. It means finding your rhythm in a village where everyone knows your business and then brings you soup to discuss it.

Alex saw it from the start. She saw that the taverna wasn't just a place for food. That the lemon grove wasn't just for lemons. That this entire messy, sunburned, *tsipouro*-scented community wasn't just a home: it was a calling.

And when the old taverna closed, it was her who said, "Let's bring it back," and I followed her. Because this woman, this force of nature, this laughing, furious, olive-picking, dance-at-midnight woman, is still the centre of everything for me.

Even when she's covered in flour and yelling about permits. Even when she's so tired she stirs her coffee with a biro, because she'll still notice if someone's limping and fetch a cushion. Even when she's been shouted at by Theodora, slipped on a rogue courgette, and accidentally set fire to the tea towel, and is in a mood – because she'll still remind me to wear a hat so I don't fry what's left of my common sense.

She has a way of seeing the best version of people, and gently – or not so gently – insisting they rise to it.

The taverna exists because of her. This book exists because of her. *I* exist, at least in my current form, because of her.

She is my Greek lesson. My local earthquake. My lighthouse. My love.

So if you ever wonder why I go along with the madness, why I agree to reopen tavernas and plant oregano and argue about cheese quotas, now you know.

It's because of Alex.

And honestly, it's always been Alex.

CHAPTER ELEVEN

THE WHISPERING TREES

After our soft opening, which had gone mostly well, all things considered, we found ourselves in a kind of holding pattern. There were no disasters. Just a few… moments.

The wine incident, for instance, had involved a tourist from Thessaloniki who misunderstood Claude's poetic flourish and opened three bottles at once "to taste the difference". He still didn't understand anything. But he tried. Valiantly.

Then there was the chair collapse: a moment of pure Greek theatre when one of the older villagers, Vangelis, sat down, heard a crack, and disappeared like a magician's assistant.

Theodora blamed Stamos for "reinforcing" the chair with an empty wine bottle. Stamos blamed the chair for being difficult. Claude wrote a poem about it.

And finally, there was the spirited debate over music. Claude insisted on a carefully curated French–Greek fusion playlist involving accordion remixes. Maria vetoed it immediately. Eleni brought out a USB stick labelled "summer bangers 2007", and somehow that's what played for the rest of the night.

Still – no one got food poisoning, three people asked to book birthdays, and one stranger told Alex it felt like "eating inside a memory". So, naturally, we were ready for the next phase.

The tables were set. The kitchen was scrubbed. The fridge had stopped humming like a tractor in its final moments. But there was one small issue. We still didn't have permission to open. It was a minefield of bureaucracy, all wrapped in plastic, filed in triplicate, and waiting on the man from the council to come back from his cousin's wedding.

But while we waited, for signatures, stamps, and whichever department was currently in charge of coastal tree shadows, we had a more immediate problem to solve: space. We needed to get on with converting the lemon grove.

Eleven wobbly tables and Spiros's immovable bench weren't going to cut it when summer truly descended. Tourists had begun circling like curious seagulls. Locals were already behaving as if Zorba's had never closed. And our seating capacity was reaching critical mass. One more chair and someone was going to end up balanced in the fig tree with a plate of calamari on their lap.

So, with Zorba's vague but essential blessing, and a pile of mismatched tables and second- or possibly third-hand chairs that Dimitri "acquired" from undisclosed sources (we didn't ask), we continued our work on the grove.

But before we could risk seating actual paying guests among the bees and wild oregano, we needed a test run. Something informal. Low-key. A soft trial to see if the trees tolerated company and if the chairs held together long enough for a meal.

Naturally, we decided to have a picnic the following day. Within an hour, the word had spread. Not officially. There weren't any posters or announcements. That would've required planning. No, this was the village method: Maria. Who told Theodora. Who told George. Who told Claude, which was a mistake, who told Eleni, who immediately told us it was illegal without the necessary forms and permission from the mayor's office, the police, the fire department and God.

But we didn't bother with any of that. By the next morning, our little test picnic had become a full-blown social event. It wasn't clear what it was about, only that it was happening.

Alex laid out some rugs under the trees. I brought out the new, second- or third-hand chairs that Dimitri had found. The ones that only wobbled if you sat too confidently.

Dimitri arrived with a bag of something freshly deceased and a charcoal grill he claimed had once been used by his uncle in Thessaloniki during the war.

Spiros did not bring his bench. Of course not. The bench stayed exactly where it had always been, just under the tree, precisely two arm-lengths from the beach, and three from the nearest source of unsolicited conversation.

Instead, Spiros brought himself, to supervise, comment, and occasionally sigh in a way that suggested everyone was doing it wrong.

Theodora brought *pastitsio* the size of a piano lid. Maria arrived in what she called "understated picnic attire", which included platform sandals and a parasol. Claude played "ethno-jazz fusion" from his phone until someone's cousin tripped over the speaker wire.

And it was perfect.

Children ran under the trees with crusts of bread. The smell of grilled fish mingled with thyme, old arguments, and new stories. Wine flowed. Someone sang. No one knew the words, but everyone joined in.

We ate. We laughed. And then Eleni asked the question.

"So," she said, with the casual precision of someone starting a war, "who now actually owns the grove?"

Cutlery froze. Chewing paused. Even the breeze gave up and sat down.

Alex cleared her throat. "Well... we found a land deed. From Zorba's uncle. Zorba has given us permission to use it provided we care for it."

"But Zorba never mentioned it before," Maria cut in, already scanning for allies. "And my aunt used to pick lemons here during the junta. That has to count for something."

Spiros took a slow drag of his cigarette and said, "It's always just been here." Which, in village terms, is both a statement of fact and a full stop on the conversation.

"Zorba said the land belongs to the people who care for it," said Dimitri, waving a grilled prawn for emphasis.

"That's what squatters say," muttered Eleni, pouring more wine.

Claude suggested a Grove Committee. The silence that followed was respectful, but very final.

Theodora interrupted by shouting that the *pastitsio* was cooling and if people didn't eat more, she'd throw it in the sea.

Alex and I exchanged the look. You know the one. The one you develop after years of marriage and navigating Greek family meals, which is to say, crises held at the dinner table with side salad.

But the grove had already spoken.

Not in words, but in that very Greek way; through glances, memories, and the casual dropping of names long buried but somehow legally significant. It wasn't a picnic any more. It was a possession ritual.

After that, things began to happen. No one announced anything, but by the next morning, the grove had been unofficially divided into zones of influence.

Maria arrived early with a notebook and a floppy hat, muttering about light quality and ideal breeze direction. When asked, she said she was "just taking some measurements for the community".

That evening, Dimitri was seen dragging a bucket into the far corner, muttering something about "restoring natural balance" and "bee diplomacy". By morning, the old vacant hives had been cleaned, reoccupied, and rearranged, flanked by three new makeshift boxes and a hand-painted sign that read, "Do not disturb: bees at work." The bees were real.

George fertilised a few lemon trees with what he claimed was "heritage goat manure". Claude set up a collapsible table, read Camus to imaginary guests, and fended off mosquitoes with lavender oil while calling it a "meditative enclave".

Theodora planted oregano with the aggressive efficiency of someone marking territory. She left behind a laminated schedule and watering instructions.

Eleni roped off a "processing area" with broken deck chairs and said she was experimenting with lemon-based soap formulas. She handed out samples.

And all the while, we waited.

For the permit. For the inspector. For something official-looking with a stamp and at least one unnecessary signature.

But the grove didn't wait. It moved on. Claimed. Cultivated. Whispered over and walked through. Quietly, mysteriously, it made its own decisions about who was allowed in and who was just visiting.

We didn't dare seat anyone there, not yet. It was sacred ground. Or at least, technically, off-limits until Eleni could convince the local office that lemon trees weren't a structural hazard.

And us? We watched. Took notes. Tended the trees. Tried not to get in the way.

"This is getting out of hand," I said one morning, as Alex returned with a basket full of oregano.

"It was never *in* hand," she replied.

And she was right. The grove didn't need paperwork. It didn't need permission. It already belonged, not to us, but to itself.

And we were just lucky just to be invited to the picnic.

CHAPTER TWELVE

THE CHEESE STANDS ALONE

George didn't say much. He didn't have to.

His wife, Theodora, had been saying things on his behalf for thirty-seven years. Loudly, thoroughly, and often in public. But George had his cheese, and that was enough.

We first met George, Theodora, and their daughter Mary the morning after the storm of the century hit our village.

The river, which had previously minded its business at the edge of our garden, had decided, in a fit of spontaneity, to change direction entirely and detour directly through our living room. Furniture floated. Rugs became islands. Our cat developed a thousand-yard stare usually seen in veterans of maritime disaster.

Alex and I stood in the ruins, surveying the scene with the dazed confusion of people trying to remember if home insurance covered acts of God, hydrological rebellion, or spiteful geography.

That's when the van pulled up.

It didn't so much park as shudder to a halt in a spray of water; a vehicle that arrived not out of transportation necessity, but sheer brilliant timing. The door flung open, and out jumped three figures carrying brooms, mops, and the unmistakable look of people on a mission.

"We've come to clean your house," Theodora announced, marching towards us as though storm recovery was simply another item on her to-do list.

Behind her was George, stoic and steady, gripping a shovel like a man who'd dug his way through worse and wasn't about to be impressed by a little indoor river. Mary followed with the air of a woman who could carry five mops, correct your cleaning technique, and still look good doing it.

There was no discussion. No polite hesitation. Just action.

Within seconds, Theodora was barking instructions, George was redirecting silt like a battlefield engineer, and Mary had opened every window, flung every door, assessed the job.

Alex and I just stood there, still in shock, holding soggy towels and wondering whether this was an emergency response team or a religious experience.

It turned out to be both. It was the people of the village. They saw a need, and arrived.

And that's how we met them: not through tea or introductions or any social convention, but through mud, floodwater, and the sheer, unshakable hospitality of people who don't ask if you need help.

They just bring a shovel and show up.

In a village where everyone has an opinion and at least three relatives on speed dial, George had quietly carved out a reputation as the most dependable man in Telios. Not because he was particularly fast, or especially helpful, but because he never said no.

He simply said, "We'll see."

Which, in Greek, can mean anything from yes, of course, to absolutely not, to I plan to die before that happens.

George's cheesemaking operation (calling it a "business" would be overselling it) was in what used to be his uncle's shed. Or possibly his cousin's garage. The lineage of the structure was unclear. What was clear was the smell: a mix of old wood, patience, and the slow tang of fermenting dairy.

He made three cheeses:

Mizithra – soft, crumbling, full of character.

Feta – tangy, soaked in brine, occasionally too salty (depending on how annoyed George had been that morning).

A third cheese – that no one could name but everyone ate.

He didn't advertise. He didn't label. He didn't even weigh. He simply handed you a small parcel wrapped in greaseproof paper and said, "This one's good." And it always was.

Things began to unravel the week before the grand relaunch of the taverna.

Theodora had requested "extra feta" for her new *spanakopita* menu. Maria had spread a rumour that a French food blogger might be coming. And Claude had declared we needed "a cheeseboard that shouts Evia". Which, in practical terms, meant: *George must make more cheese.*

So, naturally, everyone visited him on the same morning. Alex with a clipboard. Claude with a sketch. Dimitri with a bottle of home-made wine "to sweeten the negotiation".

George listened, quietly. He stirred something in a cauldron. He poked something else with a stick. Then he looked up and said, "We'll see."

Unbeknownst to most of the village, George's cheese output was determined by three things:

1. Whether the goats had cooperated that week.
2. Whether Theodora had given him peace.

3. Whether the moon was in the right phase (he never explained this, and no one dared ask).

And this week, all three were… problematic.

The goats had escaped. Twice. One had wandered into the bakery and caused a minor scandal by licking Vassiliki's emergency *bougatsa* tray.

Theodora was in what George called "a vinegar cycle", which involved banging pans louder than necessary and questioning his choice of socks.

And the moon. Well, Claude tried to explain that it was waxing gibbous, but George just squinted and said, "Feels like a cheese-break week."

By Friday, Alex was panicking, Theodora was muttering about "industrial imports", and Dimitri had offered to milk the goats himself, which thankfully no one accepted.

In the end, George delivered.

He arrived at the taverna with three buckets of cheese, a bag of herbs, and no explanation.

"Try this," he said, handing me a slice that smelled of thyme, wood smoke, and quiet defiance.

I bit in.

It was perfect.

"What's it called?" I asked.

George shrugged. "I call it 'enough.'"

He turned, walked back towards the shed, and disappeared into the trees.

Later that night, as we gathered under the fairy lights and served our first plates of *spanakopita* with George's cheese, Maria whispered to me, "You know why it tastes so good, don't you?"

I shook my head.

"Because he makes it angry. All the things he doesn't say. They go into the cheese."

I believed her.

Because in a village like ours, you can measure a man's soul in salt and milk.

And George, the quiet cheesemaker of Telios, was practically a philosopher.

One curd at a time.

Chapter Thirteen

Katerina the Goat

Some tavernas have mascots, a lazy cat, a noble dog, a faded football scarf nailed above the bar. We had Katerina. Technically a goat, unofficially a menace. Spiritually, the village's tiny, horned anarchist.

No one quite knew where she had come from. Spiros swore she was descended from a prize-winning milk line in the hills. Dimitri believed she was part-deer and once claimed she could read maps. Eleni, more poetic (or perhaps more superstitious), believed she was the reincarnation of her grandfather's second wife, back to collect gossip and settle scores.

Regardless of her origins, after Katerina appeared during our first opening, she never left.

Katerina's first official offence came while the kitchen was too busy to notice a goat. It was a busy lunch service: Theodora was at the stove, Mary was taking orders, and the courtyard was full. Madness was being managed, more or less.

Then Katerina walked into the kitchen.

She nudged open the fridge with surgical precision and ate half a tray of marinated aubergines. Theodora screamed, Claude applauded, Mary fainted. Dimitri claimed it as a new recipe.

"She's refined," he said proudly. "She only eats what's ripe."

"She ate the Tupperware," Theodora hissed.

From then on, she was everywhere. Despite repeated attempts to keep her out, Katerina proved ungovernable. She jumped fences. She slipped through gaps. She once climbed a fig tree, stared down at us like a woolly demigod, then leapt onto Claude's poetry table, for no reason anyone could identify.

Her known offences included interrupting two romantic proposals (both couples are still married, and Katerina is now a fertility omen); climbing onto the bar and licking the ouzo bottles; eating three handwritten manuscripts of Claude's philosophical essays; headbutting the tax inspector (Eleni sent her a thank-you card and a tray of baklava). She once bowed during mass. Father Evangelos insists it was intentional. She once vanished for an entire week, only to return wearing a child's sunhat and a plastic bracelet. No one asked questions. She didn't offer answers.

We tried all the anti-goat measures we could think of. Fences. Ropes. A politely worded sign in Greek, English, and emoji. Nothing worked. She always found new ways in. She once rode in on the back of Dimitri's scooter, munching lettuce and looking smug. She waited until no one was watching. She befriended children. She somehow got her hoofprint on an official permit.

After a while, we stopped resisting. Katerina wasn't in the taverna. She was the taverna.

One morning, Zorba arrived early, as he always did. He found Katerina asleep on his usual chair. He stared at her for a long time. Then, without a word, he dragged over another chair, sat down, and poured two *tsipouros*, one for him, one for her. She didn't move.

He raised his glass. "To troublemakers," he said. From that day on, Katerina was officially untouchable.

Later that summer, a travel journalist arrived. He came with a linen notebook and a Dictaphone.

"I'm here," he told us, "to uncover the *true heart* of Greece."

He tried to interview Claude. Claude responded with three hours of Camus and a brief interpretive dance about rural despair. The journalist began to tremble. Then Katerina walked in. She sniffed his notes, sneezed on his recorder, and promptly sat on his lap.

He tried to shift her. She bit his pen. Later, he published an article entitled "The Goat Who Knows Too Much".

It went mildly viral. The photos were mostly of hooves.

Now, she has her own spot in the lemon grove – a shady patch of grass where no one sits without permission. She eats what she likes and sleeps where she pleases. Children adore her. Tourists film her. Spiros pretends to hate her but once gave her his last *koulouri*. We find her in the pantry, on the roof, or occasionally in someone's car. But we don't mind any more.

Because every Greek taverna needs a little chaos. A little wilderness. Something that can't be explained, managed, or planned.

Something like Katerina.

CHAPTER FOURTEEN

Enter the Matriarch

Just when we thought the taverna was full – full of people (still not "customers" of course… not yet), full of drama, full of goats – the universe decided to give us a little something extra.

A mother.

Theodora's mother.

Her name was Kyriaki, but she would only answer to *Mana*. Not "mama", not "*yiayia*", and definitely not "Mrs" anything. Just *Mana*. Capitalised, in italics, and pronounced with the weight of seven generations of culinary authority.

Zorba's Parthenon - A Taverna by the Sea

She arrived one Tuesday morning without warning, fanfare, or luggage – just a basket of preserved lemons, a rolled-up apron, and an expression that suggested she'd seen too many cities and not enough grilled lamb lately.

"I've had enough of Crete," she announced, placing her handbag on the taverna counter. "It's full of tourists and people who can't tell a proper *avgolemono* from a boiled insult."

We blinked. Theodora turned pale. George turned invisible.

"Mana," Theodora said, slowly, as though trying not to startle a bear, "what brings you here?"

"I missed the village," said Mana. "I missed the sea. And I missed my kitchen."

Theodora's eyes twitched. "Your kitchen is in your home in Chania."

"It was. Now it's wherever you're overcooking the *stifado*." There was a silence so sharp it sliced through the smell of roasting peppers.

She wore black from head to toe, not out of mood, but tradition. In Greece, widows wear black as a tribute to their deceased husbands. Some wear it for a few months, a gesture of respect. Others, like her, wear it for the rest of their lives, as if mourning had become part of the wardrobe of the soul.

Within ten minutes, Mana had found an empty stool, adjusted it twice, and claimed her permanent position in the corner of the kitchen. From that moment on, she sat there every day, not working, not serving, just *supervising*.

"You have too much salt in that," she said, nodding at Theodora's soup.

"I haven't added any yet," Theodora replied.

"Exactly."

She did not lift a pan, but no dish escaped her commentary. If something turned out delicious, she smiled sweetly and said, "Ah, she remembered how I showed her."

If something was undercooked: "She never listens. Even as a child. Always rushing."

Claude attempted to greet her in French. She ignored him. Dimitri offered her a shot of *tsipouro*. She sniffed it, gave a short nod, and said, "Acceptable." Then she added, "Needs more cloves."

Maria tried to out-gossip her. She lost.

Alex whispered, "We've got another Theodora."

"She's worse," Theodora hissed back. "She *made* me."

George offered to build her a bench outside, "for the sea air." She refused. "The food is *inside*."

Spiros gave her one long look, then lit a cigarette and muttered, "We need stronger wine."

Katerina the goat tried to eat her shawl. Mana swatted her on the nose with a spoon and said, "No." Katerina backed off. Everyone backed off. We all agreed not to mess with Mana.

One night, we had a full taverna. The kitchen was in uproar. Theodora was six orders deep in stuffed tomatoes.

Mana, perched on her stool, watched like a hawk judging a soap opera.

Finally, Theodora snapped.

"Do you want to cook it yourself?"

"No," Mana said, calm as thunder. "If I wanted to cook, I'd go back to Chania. I just don't want you to ruin the family name."

Claude whispered, "I think I'm in love."

Maria whispered, "I think she *is* Theodora."

Alex said, "I'm putting her name on the rota. Just to scare Theodora into being early."

That night, when the last table was cleared and the taverna was finally quiet, Mana stood, dusted off her apron (which had never been used), and turned to Theodora.

"You did well," she said. "But don't get comfortable," she added. "Standards must be maintained."

And with that, she left… only to return the next morning at 7:03 a.m. with a bag of wild greens and a critique of our coffee. Now we had three culinary queens. A trinity of taste, terror, and unsolicited advice. And heaven help the fool who questioned the seasoning.

***

It was bound to happen eventually.

Not a clash, more of a convergence.

Two elemental presences. One bowl of olives. And a quiet agreement forged without a single word.

Mana brought her own olives. From Crete, of course. She didn't trust ours, said they were "too cheerful." Hers were grown on a cousin's land near Rethymno, harvested at dawn during a full moon, brined in sea salt, garlic, and what she described only as "*something special*".

No one asked what that meant.

She sat at her usual perch near the kitchen, a bowl beside her, gently crushing each olive between her thumb and forefinger before tasting and occasionally muttering, "This batch needs more wind."

Katerina approached, slowly, eyes locked on the bowl. She stopped just short of Mana's feet.

Mana looked down. Katerina looked up. For a moment, the whole taverna held its breath.

Mana picked up an olive. She held it out. Katerina sniffed it.

Then, in an act that would echo through village legend, Mana said, simply, "Sit."

And Katerina, Goddess of Chaos, Enemy of Order, Eater of Menus and Forms – *sat*.

Mana nodded once and gave her the olive.

Katerina chewed it thoughtfully. Then she headbutted the leg of Mana's stool in what we later interpreted as polite approval. From that moment, a strange peace emerged.

Katerina no longer tried to raid the kitchen when Mana

was present. And Mana, in turn, began saving "the chewy ones" just for her.

Theodora was appalled. "You've trained the goat."

"No," Mana said. "We've reached an understanding."

"They say goats can't be reasoned with."

"Only amateurs say that."

From then on, Katerina spent much of her time parked beside Mana's stool, occasionally licking her apron or stealing stray grape leaves. And Mana would cluck her tongue and say, "She's better company than half the tourists."

And we adjusted. Because at Zorba's, if a goat and a grandmother can form an alliance, anything is possible.

And yes, Claude tried to write a poem about it. Katerina ate it.

CHAPTER FIFTEEN

Dimitri and the Church of Storms

Father Evangelos was a man of infinite gentleness.

He moved through the village like a warm breeze, never causing ripples, never causing offence, simply smoothing the wrinkles of daily life with a smile and a soft blessing. He understood the island mentality better than most born to it.

And he loved it: the arguments, the contradictions, the confusion wrapped around kindness like vines around an olive tree.

But even Father Evangelos had a secret.

It had been a moment so bizarre, so utterly Greek, that it lodged itself into village legend, passed along in whispers and knowing chuckles, growing slightly with every retelling.

Technically, it's a secret between Father Evangelos and Dimitri.

But of course, Maria heard about it.

Which means the whole village knows it now, embroidered, embellished, and considered absolute gospel.

It all started, as many things do in Greece, with a plan that was not entirely legal and not entirely thought through. Dimitri, our resident odd-job man, hunter, fisherman, philosopher, and opportunist, had heard rumours of a new fish farm across the straits. A veritable paradise of fat, lazy fish penned in like sheep.

To Dimitri's mind, it was simple. Why sit in a boat all night, throwing his trident at uncooperative fish and arguing with the moon, when he could simply borrow a few fish that nobody would miss?

It was not, he reasoned, theft. It was more... *redistribution of aquatic resources.*

Armed with his trident, a coil of rope, and a worrying lack of maps, he set off at night in his battered little boat, its engine a heroic 4 horsepower if you believed the label and were feeling generous.

He hugged the rocky coast of Evia Island, slipping past darkened headlands, planning to cross towards Volos and the new fish farms by dawn.

But as Dimitri passed the last sheltering cliffs, the weather changed. Suddenly. Violently.

The calm, glassy sea he had slipped across turned wild – a living thing with teeth.

A fierce northern wind, roaring straight down from Mount Pelion, slammed into him broadside.

The sea went from gentle ripples to mountains in minutes.

The waves lifted his tiny boat like a cork, spun it, and shoved it backwards, out into open water.

His little engine screamed bravely against the wind, but it was hopeless.

Dimitri was caught, helpless, tossed back into the middle of the straits. The rain lashed sideways. Lightning crackled over the black cliffs. The world shrank to a howling dark tunnel of fear, salt, and blinding white flashes.

Dimitri, who was no stranger to foolishness, was also no stranger to survival. He made a decision, the first smart one of the night: *go with the storm*. Let the wind drive him wherever it wanted, as long as it was towards land.

Somewhere, somehow, he would find safety.

Hours passed.

The world was all roar and blackness. Dimitri's hands were numb, his clothes soaked, his little boat half-swamped with icy water.

And then, through the darkness, he saw it.

A flickering light. Faint. Far away, but steady, calling him home like a beacon.

With the last sputtering cough of his engine and the last flickers of his strength, Dimitri steered towards it. Closer and closer.

The light grew brighter.

Finally, miraculously, he ground onto a narrow strip of rocky beach. The boat thudded against the stones, and he half-stumbled, half-crawled ashore. The beach was rough and wild, framed by black cliffs.

But the light was real, swinging gently above the doorway of a tiny, weather-beaten church, clinging stubbornly to the rocks. God's lighthouse, if ever there was one.

Dimitri hauled the boat above the tide line, tying it to a battered tree with shaking hands. Then he staggered up towards the light.

The door creaked open easily. Inside: darkness. The candle above the door flickered low.

Dimitri unhooked it carefully and held it aloft, peering into the gloom.

Stone walls. A few rough benches. The smell of wax and old incense. No one there. Just the heavy, timeless silence of Greek churches, the sense that even the dust mites are holding their breath.

Dimitri, half-dead with exhaustion, laid the lamp down by the altar and sank down onto the stone floor.

The last thing he thought, before sleep dragged him

under, was, "Clearly, God has already forgiven me for trying to steal fish."

He drifted in a strange, grey space. Dreams and reality tangled. He was back in the storm. He was home. He was nowhere.

Unknown to Dimitri, the body of a deceased fisherman had been laid out in the tiny, whitewashed church, resting beneath a modest shroud, awaiting burial the next morning. It was tradition, a final night spent among incense and candlelight, where the soul might linger and the villagers could come to pay their respects between dinner and gossip.

Father Evangelos arrived just after midnight. The air outside was still, the cicadas momentarily quiet. Inside, the church glowed faintly from a flickering oil lamp suspended over the altar, the kind of light that throws shadows which move when you're not looking.

He entered gently, respectfully, his shoes soft against the stone floor. He had come, as priests do, to check the candles, say a quiet prayer, and perhaps have a final word with the man who now belonged more to heaven than to Evia.

But something felt… off.

A breeze moved when it shouldn't have. The shadows didn't quite hold still. There was, unmistakably, breathing.

Then, again, closer now.

He raised his candle, not knowing what to expect. He asked the corpse a question. "Dimitri, are you sleeping well, my friend?"

The voice was gentle. Warm. Kind. Otherworldly.

"Yes… I slept very well," came the reply.

A pause. A long, holy pause. And then a scream. A high-pitched, unexpected, soul-shattering *scream* that bounced off every fresco and icon in the church.

Father Evangelos flung the door open with the force of divine panic and sprinted into the night, cassock flapping behind him like a startled bat, sandals slapping the stones as though chased by a thousand demons.

Dimitri jerked upright. The candle had gone out.

The church was dark, but dim light still leaked through the cracks in the door.

And there, by the altar, he saw the coffin. A rough wooden coffin. Open. And inside it, a body.

The face was peaceful, familiar somehow, like looking into a mirror distorted by age and sorrow.

Pinned to the side of the coffin, scrawled in uneven hand, were the words: "Dimitrios Papadakis. Beloved Fisherman. Rest in Peace."

Dimitri blinked. The name was his. Or close enough to make no difference to a tired, storm-tossed brain. For a long moment, he stood frozen, caught between laughter and panic.

Had he died?

Was this a warning?

Had God lured him ashore just to show him what his end would look like, alone, anonymous, a weather-beaten old soul in a cracked wooden box?

Or maybe, just maybe, it was simply Greece, where the line between the living and the dead, the sacred and the absurd, is as thin and flickering as a candle in a storm.

As the sun rose, Father Evangelos came back.

Dimitri was sitting on the bench outside the church, pale as communion linen and sipping water from a plastic bottle with both hands like it might shatter if he let go. His eyes were wide, unfocused, but his mouth was grinning – the kind of grin you only see on people who've either seen God or been struck by lightning, or possibly both.

Father Evangelos emerged quietly from behind a rock, robes fluttering slightly in the breeze. He paused for a moment, took in the sight before him, and then sat beside Dimitri without a word.

They didn't speak. Not at first. There was nothing to say that wouldn't have sounded ridiculous, even in a village where half the men have seen ghosts and the other half have married them.

Eventually, after a long silence, Father Evangelos placed a gentle hand on Dimitri's shoulder. "Second resurrection?" he asked softly.

Dimitri shook his head slowly, as if even that simple movement might trigger divine consequences. "I thought I'd died," he said. "I thought I'd been taken."

Father Evangelos nodded. "You were in the presence of something sacred."

"Sacred," Dimitri agreed. "Or very, very illegal."

Another long pause.

Then, unexpectedly, Father Evangelos chuckled, a soft, wheezy laugh, like air escaping an old accordion. "I missed the first resurrection," he said. "And it seems I missed the second one, too."

They sat there together, two men bound by a shared silence and something neither was quite ready to explain.

Finally, Dimitri looked down and whispered, "I didn't speak to God, you know."

"I know," said Father Evangelos. "But I'll bless you anyway."

They nodded in unison, both men of few words and many thoughts. And in that quiet agreement, it was settled. The night would not be spoken of again. Not in sermons. Not in *kafeneio* gossip. Not even in the bakery queue.

And technically, *technically*, it wasn't.

But Maria found out, of course.

And from there, the story grew wings, sprouted roots, gathered speed. Today, it lives as one of the great village legends: Dimitri: the man who spent a night in a coffin, confessed his sins to a ghost, and came back to tell the tale, slightly wetter, slightly wiser, and no less likely to steal a fish if the opportunity arises.

Of course, it was only a matter of time before Dimitri told the story himself.

And naturally, by the time he did, the facts had evolved somewhat.

We were sitting at the taverna one afternoon, the sea sparkling, the air warm, the coffee cups dangerously close to becoming *tsipouro* cups, when Dimitri launched into it.

"I was out there," he said, jabbing a finger at the horizon, "battling a storm the size of Mount Olympus. A real typhoon."

George, ever the practical one, muttered, "You were probably battling indigestion."

Dimitri ignored him. "My boat was upside down, my engine had exploded twice, and I was fighting off sea monsters."

Maria gasped theatrically.

Claude sipped his wine and suggested that perhaps they were symbolic sea monsters, representing Dimitri's guilty conscience.

Dimitri gave Claude a look usually reserved for tax inspectors. "Anyway," he pressed on, "I saw a light! A holy light! Sent by Saint Nicholas himself! It guided me to shore, straight to a church!"

He paused dramatically.

"And inside…" he said, voice dropping to a hoarse whisper, "I saw my own funeral."

There was a collective intake of breath.

"Open coffin. Candle burning. A voice calling my name from the beyond!"

At this point, Dimitri crossed himself so violently he nearly knocked over the salt shaker.

"And I realised, the message was clear: Change my ways! Fish honestly! Live purely!"

There was a long, respectful pause. Then Zorba snorted so hard he nearly inhaled an olive.

"Next day," Zorba said dryly, "Dimitri was back at the harbour selling fish that still had barcodes stuck to them."

The table erupted in laughter.

Even Father Evangelos, sitting quietly in the shade, allowed himself a small smile.

Dimitri shrugged, completely unfazed.

"Eh," he said. "Saint Nicholas understands. Survival first, confessions later."

And with that, he poured himself another coffee, heavy on the sugar, light on the repentance, and the story, already half-legend, grew just a little taller.

CHAPTER SIXTEEN

THE GRAND REOPENING (TAKE TWO)

It was a Tuesday that began like most others: warm sun, mild upheaval, and Claude describing the breeze as "existential". We were still unofficially open, still serving not-customers for not-money, still waiting for the permits that would turn our lovely act of taverna theatre into a legal business.

And then Eleni burst through the kitchen door waving a piece of paper like she was leading a revolution.

"I have it!" she shouted, breathless and glowing with triumph. "The permit!"

We all froze.

"You mean *a* permit?" I asked cautiously.

"No," she said, eyes wild. "*The* permit. With all the stamps. All the signatures. Even the official smell." We gathered around like villagers receiving the lost scrolls. There it was.

Stamped, dated, and, in at least three places, slightly smudged. Permission. To open. Officially.

The document was printed on the usual municipal parchment, with Greek text that seemed to have been translated from another language, possibly under duress. But it was real. Eleni had navigated the bureaucratic labyrinth with the single-mindedness of a woman who once pushed her father's pickup truck into the sea over a family squabble.

Alex stared at it for a long moment. Then she smiled, the quiet, unstoppable kind of smile that usually meant I was about to be roped into something dangerous.

"It's time," she said.

I looked at the sagging pergola, the slightly singed menu board, and Dimitri attempting to teach a confused Canadian how to gut a fish with a bread knife.

Alex narrowed her eyes at me. "Optimism, Peter. Optimism and duct tape and fishing line. That's what keeps Greece running." She wasn't wrong. But, this time, she said, we would have:

- Properly printed menus (with fewer spelling errors).

- A set menu (because last time, everyone ordered something different, and half of them wanted it "just like my mother makes").
- A priest to bless the taverna officially.
- Live music – if Dimitri's cousin's bouzouki didn't explode.
- No goats.

That last point was stressed particularly heavily.

Meanwhile, the village buzzed with excitement. Maria was already circulating invitations via word-of-mouth (and several accidental exaggerations involving a "famous guest" who turned out to be Spiros's nephew from Patras). Claude insisted on designing a "simple but elegant" floral display, which ended up looking suspiciously like a bridal arch. Vassiliki baked like a woman possessed. Eleni filed two extra permits just in case. Stamos fixed the wobbly tables (mostly by moving them slightly and declaring them "better balanced by the moon's gravity").

And in the background, always there but almost forgotten in the rush, the lemon grove whispered quietly in the breeze.

It was, by all accounts, going to be the event of the season. Weeks of planning, arguments, building, fixing, baking, debates, and frantic repairs, plus a few conveniently overlooked regulations, culminated in the taverna's grand opening. Almost. Tables were arranged (some level, others delightfully wobbly).

The lights twinkled (half disco, half dark). The fridge groaned like a wounded beast, but the contents were cold, so we deemed it "operational".

Alex stood at the door with a clipboard and a terrifying sense of optimism. I stood beside her, already sweating through my best shirt.

"It's going to be fine," she said.

"Yes," I lied.

At first, it was almost peaceful. The sun sank gently behind the hills, melting into streaks of lavender and rust. The first customers, mostly villagers who were already involved in the taverna anyway, arrived with smiles, casseroles, and wine bottles that had suspiciously handwritten labels.

In Greece, hospitality is a two-way performance. You bring something – sweets, wine, sometimes an entire casserole. Even if you're headed to a place that's literally serving you dinner. Tradition doesn't argue with logic. It just brings more food.

Claude flitted between tables, adjusting napkins, muttering "ambiance, ambiance" under his breath like a French spell. Maria was stationed by the front with a welcome drink and the latest gossip. Spiros had appointed himself head of security and was positioned under the olive tree on his bench, cigarette in his mouth. George was restocking the wine rack while taste-testing each bottle, "for quality control". The *tsipouro* was still banned, though Dimitri kept sipping it under the table, "for quality control". Apparently, "quality control" was becoming the official village excuse for drinking before noon.

The taverna resembled a theatre troupe on the brink of a mutiny. One without a script. Or a stage. Or a fire-safety certificate. The wine had exploded again. Claude's lighting installation had collapsed twice. And Eleni had started using words like "unconstitutional seating plans" and "lemon-zoning violations".

Vassiliki threatened to go on a baking strike unless someone "did something about the aura". Maria announced that a blogger from Thessaloniki might show up, and demanded we invent a hashtag. Stamos discovered a second, smaller goat in the storage shed. No one asked how it got there. We were too tired to care.

Alex hadn't blinked in hours – she stared ahead like a woman who'd seen too much *Big Brother* and not enough coffee.

"Tonight," she said, in the voice of someone who once convinced an entire ferry crew to delay departure because the captain's aunt had just delivered still-warm galaktoboureko and it would have been rude not to stay for dessert, "we open."

A pause.

"Even if Dimitri's fish start singing."

Dimitri looked up, hopeful. "Can they do that?" Alex glared. Dimitri returned to gutting something vaguely aquatic. I just stood back and watched this slow-moving miracle take shape: Uneven tables. Mismatched chairs. Wild lemon trees whispering in the dark. It was beautiful. It was doomed. It was ours.

For a while, everything ran as it should. The sun stayed up. The goat stayed out of the kitchen. Even Dimitri stayed, long enough to scale three fish, deliver four unsolicited opinions, and then mysteriously vanish sometime after lunch.

By late afternoon, the fish delivery still hadn't arrived. When we called him, Dimitri sounded unusually breathless. "Broken rudder," he said. "And a small fire." Alex asked what was on fire. "Mostly just my pride," he replied. And hung up.

No fish meant we were down a third of the menu.

Then the oven went out. Just like that. One moment Theodora was sliding in a tray of stuffed peppers, the next she was shouting ancient curses at an appliance that had apparently decided to retire mid-shift. Stamos, sensing an opportunity to wield a wrench and his usual misplaced confidence, began tinkering. He crawled under the counter, muttered things like "Ah yes, definitely thermal flux," and finally emerged holding a chewed piece of rubber like it was a sacred relic. "Found the problem," he declared. "Goat." And sure enough, the gas hose was now a half-eaten spiral of rubber. Somewhere nearby, Katerina chewed her cud with the serene satisfaction of a saboteur who had struck again, leaving us oven-less.

Within ten minutes, the lights flickered, the ice machine coughed once and died, and the toilet began flushing with what sounded like a tuba solo.

Maria began spreading rumours that the fish delay was actually due to sabotage from the next village, or more likely, the Turks.

Vassiliki arrived with two trays of emergency pastries and told us all to stop panicking and eat something.

Alex was still smiling. That was worrying.

At seven o'clock sharp, the real guests began to arrive.

Not just locals. Tourists. Holidaymakers. The mayor (invited or not). Two people from the regional tourism board who had heard about the "cultural revival project" and brought brochures.

We were officially in trouble.

The tables were full. The staff – except for Alex – were panicking. The wine was flowing in three directions, only one of which was intentional.

Claude had set up a corner for poetry readings. The microphone didn't work, so he read louder. George started pouring ouzo like water. Theodora and Mary were shouting at each other in the kitchen, which is usually a good sign.

And I stood in the middle of it all, blinking slowly, wondering how on earth this had happened, and how, somehow, it was also sort of working.

Naturally, the power went out, at the peak of service. The fridge gave one final sigh and surrendered. The lights died. The music stopped. The taverna was plunged into warm, wine-scented darkness.

There was a long pause.

Then someone started clapping. A child giggled. Zorba raised his glass from his shadowy corner and shouted, "Well, at least now no one can see the prices!"

Laughter broke out like a wave. Candles appeared. Phones lit up faces. Someone strummed a *bouzouki*. Claude began singing a slow, sad French love song that sounded bizarrely beautiful in the candlelight.

By the end of the evening, it was clear we were no longer running a restaurant. We were hosting a gathering. A moment. A memory being born.

The food was late.

Someone – and we're looking directly at *you*, Dimitri – blamed Poseidon.

The wine ran out.

Because we grossly underestimated the collective thirst of Theodora, George, and Claude's inexplicably large extended French-speaking fan club who treated rosé like holy water.

The bathroom flooded.

Because Stamos had "improved the plumbing" using an old snorkel, two mismatched garden hoses, and what may have been part of a washing machine from 1983.

And yet, nobody left. They stayed. They laughed. They passed around a mop bucket and declared it "symbolic".

Instead:

They talked.

They argued (as is custom).

They laughed (also custom).

They danced (at one point with a chair). Alex danced on

the table. So did the goat.

Someone tried to teach an Austrian tourist the *syrtaki* using Claude's scarf as a demonstration prop.

At least two couples rekindled old romances.

One octopus went missing.

The stars came out. The sea whispered against the sand like it was eavesdropping.

I raised a chipped glass of warm, slightly oxidised *retsina* and shouted, "To the taverna!"

And everyone, everyone, even Eleni, cheered.

Alex, standing beside me in the dark, her cheeks flushed with sun, wine, and dangerous levels of success, turned to me with a grin that could have lit the coastline.

"This," she said, arms wide, eyes sparkling, "is perfect."

I looked around, at the wine-stained tablecloths, the off-tune mandolin player, the small child trying to eat a candle, and nodded.

Because it was.

Not clean. Not smooth. Not remotely according to plan. But perfect in that uniquely Greek way. Beautiful. Chaotic. A little sticky. Held together by cracked chairs, questionable wiring, divine laughter, and the kind of hope that refuses to check the receipts.

We hadn't just opened a taverna.

We'd brought something back to life. And now, there was no turning back.

Zorba's Parthenon - A Taverna by the Sea

At the end of the night, Zorba shuffled over.

He surveyed the mess, the spilled wine, the half-burnt candles, the faint smell of the fish that never arrived.

"You'll need a new fridge," he said.

"Yes," I agreed.

"And a better electrician."

"Definitely."

He nodded, sucked on his cigarette, and looked out towards the sea.

Then, without turning, he said, "Still... you opened. And you made them stay."

He handed me a bottle of *tsipouro* – old, cloudy, and slightly warm.

"Drink this. You've earned it."

And Zorba walked off into the dark, our taverna glowing behind him, alive again.

CHAPTER SEVENTEEN

THE MORNING AFTER

We had finally opened. And somehow, we had survived.

And now, in the soft light of morning, with the sea gently lapping the sand and the sun climbing sleepily over the hills, we were left with the aftermath.

The taverna looked like it had hosted a small civil war. Chairs were scattered like forgotten thoughts.

Wine bottles lay empty, some still upright, some looking like they'd tried to escape and given up halfway. A half-eaten pastry was perched on the *bouzouki*. Claude swore it had cultural significance. Dimitri was asleep under a table, using a crate of lemons as a pillow. He snored softly, like a contented piglet. At some point during the night, he'd lost one shoe and gained an earring.

Maria arrived first.

She took one look around, sighed deeply, then smiled.

"Well," she said, picking up a napkin with the disdain of someone handling biohazard, "that went better than expected."

She then leaned in and whispered, conspiratorially, "By the way, I heard the Minister for Culture was here. Incognito. Sat in the back. Ate three sardines. Said it was 'deeply authentic.'"

Alex arched an eyebrow. "Maria… there were no sardines."

Maria shrugged. "There were for him."

And just like that, another rumour was born.

By mid-morning, the village began to arrive, broom-wielding, groggy, cheerful. Stamos brought tools and fixed nothing. George brewed coffee strong enough to revive the dead. Theodora immediately began reorganising the kitchen and muttering about "standards". Claude lit incense and declared it "a cleansing ritual". Zorba supervised from his usual chair, issuing critiques with the authority of a retired admiral. Father Evangelos came by with a blessing and a box of pastries. Spiros brought more *tsipouro*, just in case the clean-up got emotional.

And me?

I mostly tried not to step in anything sticky.

As we worked, something unexpected settled over the place: calm.

Not silence, never that. But the kind of shared peace that comes after chaos. After doing something hard, badly, together, and somehow making it beautiful.

We laughed at the night's disasters. We compared hangovers. We found someone's missing glasses in the ice bucket.

At one point, Alex stopped scrubbing a wine stain from the table and looked around, the people, the mess, the sunshine, the sea. "This," she said, "was the point all along."

I nodded. Still sticky. Still proud.

Just before noon, Dimitri stirred under his table, blinking like a mole. He stretched, sat up, and said, perfectly seriously, "Did I give the Minister of Culture a fish?"

Everyone turned. Maria smiled sweetly. "Of course you did, Dimitri."

He nodded, satisfied, and lay back down.

And that's how the story of the Grand Reopening ended, with crumbs on the floor, laughter in the air, and one very confused fisherman dreaming of government recognition. The taverna had reopened.

I wandered to the edge of the grove. The lemons gleamed pale and quiet under the sun. Imperfect. Wild. Poised.

The lemon grove had found its family and would soon be part of the story. And somehow, despite bureaucracy and broken chairs and exploding wine barrels, the village, *our* village, had reminded itself what mattered.

Not the rules. Not the profits. Not perfect floors or straight pergolas. It was the people.

The stories. The stubborn, ridiculous, wonderful love that held it all together. Life in Greece isn't neat. It isn't tidy. It's crooked. It's cracked. It's full of goats and gossip and lemon trees that refuse to die. And it's beautiful. Exactly as it is.

CHAPTER EIGHTEEN

SPIROS AND THE TOBACCO POLICE

In every village, there are unwritten laws stronger than anything written on paper.

You might think that in a small seaside taverna with mismatched chairs and tables that wobble like Bambi on ice, people would just sit wherever they were told.

You would be wrong.

In the world of Greek village tavernas, *where you sit* is a reflection of your social standing, your marital history, your fishing reputation, and in at least one case, your grandfather's involvement in a 1972 cheese theft.

Maria preferred to sit *in view of the door*, but not too close to it, and only if she could face the kitchen. This, she explained, was "for energy flow". Which sounded suspiciously like feng shui until she added, "And also in case Theodora burns something."

George preferred to sit far enough from the grill to avoid smoke, but close enough to be considered "within meat range". Claude liked to sit under a tree, but only that tree, because the leaves reminded him of Provence. Dimitri sat wherever his plate landed, usually barefoot and already chewing something.

The tourists had begun by sitting near the edge, by the sea, which sounds romantic until you realise it's also where the wind is strongest, and the table legs sink into the sand like slowly drowning furniture. So, they had gradually moved to the tables under the lemon trees.

Spiros, naturally, had his bench. This was never up for negotiation. Tourists who attempted to sit there were gently redirected with a look so powerful it could curdle milk.

Of course, in our village, everyone smoked. It didn't matter whether Spiros sat outside under the olive tree puffing away, or on rainy days, under the pergola on his reserve bench. The first law of the village was simple: "Spiros smokes."

It didn't matter what the European Union said. It didn't matter what Athens decreed. It didn't even matter what the small print on the cigarette packets shrieked about cancer and early death.

Spiros smoked.

A few years ago, the great no-smoking edict descended upon Greece from the heavens, or, more accurately, from Brussels.

No smoking inside cafés.

No smoking inside tavernas.

No smoking anywhere except possibly in the middle of a wheat field surrounded by fire extinguishers.

Naturally, Greece immediately complied. Signs were printed. Rules were posted. Every taverna window, every café table, proudly displayed a fresh "No Smoking" sticker.

Right next to the ashtrays.

I had given up smoking myself several years earlier. Six years, seven months, twenty-three days, and seven minutes earlier, not that anyone's counting.

I've never missed it. Except twice an hour. And in my dreams. And every time I order coffee, beer, wine, or even an ice cream.

But otherwise, no, I never missed it at all.

Somewhere in my brain, common sense shouts that it's a disgusting, deadly habit. Meanwhile, my subconscious continues to whisper seductively, *Just one won't hurt. One little cigarette. Think of the poetry*!

So far, I remain clear. But Spiros? Spiros had no such conflicts.

Nobody actually knows how old Spiros is. Not even Spiros. He remembers the war. He remembers the famine. He probably remembers Atlantis, if you asked him on a good day. What is certain is this: Spiros has been chain-smoking since before chain-smoking was invented. He could roll a cigarette before he could spell his own name, and still, to this day, he is never seen without a slim, hand-rolled cigarette dangling from his bottom lip like a permanent accessory.

"Listen," he growls if anyone dares comment, "I'm old. I've smoked all my life. Nobody's going to tell me when to stop. It's none of their damn business."

This is said with the force of a man who has survived world wars, government changes, and at least two café owners who tried to switch to imported coffee or serve *tsipouro* with printed labels.

Spiros, in other words, was immovable.

The signs could go up. The EU could issue all the fines it wanted. But Spiros would keep smoking.

And, somehow, the village would keep letting him.

Normally, life carried on in its glorious Greek contradiction. Signs on the window. Ashtrays on the tables. Everyone pretending not to see the smoke curling around the wine glasses. Until one rainy afternoon, a black government car rumbled into the square.

Out stepped two men in dark suits, armed with clipboards, stern expressions, and the righteous authority of minor bureaucrats on a mission. It was the Tobacco Police.

They fanned out across the village like a pair of confused

bloodhounds, peering into cafés, inspecting signs, and sniffing suspiciously at air that smelled, as it always did, of coffee, garlic, cigarette smoke, and occasional goat.

The whole village went still. A dropped spoon clattered like a gunshot. Theodora made the sign of the cross behind the counter. Vassiliki muttered darkly into her apron. George disappeared so quickly you'd have thought someone had rung the fire bell.

But Spiros sat on his reserve bench under the pergola, rolling another cigarette with calm, deliberate defiance.

The Tobacco Police spotted him instantly. They zeroed in, clipboards trembling with excitement.

One pointed dramatically at the lit cigarette. The other began quoting regulations about fines, health codes, and public safety.

Spiros looked up slowly, took a long drag, and exhaled thoughtfully into the pristine air. Then, in the most patient, reasonable tone imaginable, he said, "Son… if I stopped now, it would probably kill me."

There was a long, loaded silence.

The younger of the two inspectors, who couldn't have been more than twenty-five and was still young enough to believe in things like rules, opened his mouth to argue.

The older one, wiser, heavier, with the deadened eyes of a man who had once tried to enforce recycling bins in Crete, gently put a hand on his shoulder. "Come on," he said. "This one's exempt."

And just like that, the Tobacco Police moved on. Officially, there was no smoking in the village. The rules were respected. The forms were filled out. But Spiros kept smoking. As he always had. As he always would.

Because sometimes, just sometimes, on a good day, with a slightly flexible bureaucrat, the soul of a village is more important than the rules. Especially when that soul smells faintly of tobacco and home-made *tsipouro*.

Later that afternoon, after the drama had faded and the village had returned to its usual rhythm of coffee, gossip, and Katerina the goat wandering into inappropriate places, Spiros shuffled over to my table. He had that particular glint in his eye, the one that usually meant trouble or wisdom, and often both. Without a word, he pulled a cigarette from behind his ear, carefully hand-rolled, slightly lopsided, and smelling faintly of sea salt and old adventures.

He held it out to me.

"A gift," he said gruffly. "For your good health."

I stared at it, that crooked little offering, and felt a thousand memories stir. Six years, seven months, twenty-three days, and forty-two minutes of stubbornness and common sense wobbled dangerously in the breeze.

One cigarette.

What harm could it do?

Just one.

The world seemed to narrow, to shrink down to the tiny,

crumpled tube of paper and tobacco and the grin of an old man who had outlived every warning label ever printed.

I smiled, a little sadly, a little triumphantly, and shook my head.

"No, thank you," I said. "I'm saving myself for the next opening night."

Spiros laughed: a deep, warm sound like old wood creaking in the sun.

He shrugged, popped the cigarette back behind his ear, and shuffled away, smoke curling behind him like a signature in the air.

And just like that, temptation passed.

For now.

Because this is Greece.

And there will always be another coffee.

Another conversation.

Another chance to say yes, or no, or maybe just this once. But probably never.

CHAPTER NINETEEN

DIMITRI'S BIG IDEA

Dimitri didn't ease into things. He arrived like a thunderstorm on a clear day, loud, sudden, and suspiciously wet. There was no plan. There was no meeting. There was no calendar entry.

There was, instead, a bucket labelled "Drinkable (probably)", a bag of poorly photocopied flyers flapping in the breeze like miniature distress signals, and Dimitri zipping through the village on his ancient scooter – one hand steering, the other wildly smearing glue onto any surface that didn't move fast enough to escape. Which included, at one point, a German tourist and the church bell.

The flyers read:

TSIPOURO NIGHT AT ZORBA'S TAVERNA!
Live Music (probably) | Free Entry (definitely) | Starts at Sunset (ish)

WARNING: Not suitable for children, adults, or the cautious.

I found him halfway through defacing Spiros's bench, smoothing the flyer down with the back of a sardine tin.

"Dimitri," I said carefully, "what exactly are you doing?"

"Marketing," he replied with the enthusiasm of a man launching a tech startup, not an illegal village drinking festival. "We need a crowd."

"For what?"

He grinned. "Science. And national pride. Also, I had leftover lemons."

Back at the taverna, Maria was waving a flyer like she'd caught him embezzling.

"Why didn't I know about this?" she hissed, already composing a breaking-news bulletin for the bakery.

"It's… spontaneous," I offered.

She glared. "Spontaneity is how the village nearly burned down in 2022. And we're still banned from burning wood."

Claude arrived moments later, barefoot and beaming, tambourine in hand, draped in a scarf that appeared to be made of curtains. "Shall I prepare something from Camus?"

"No," said Alex flatly.

Then Dimitri arrived, drunk on his own confidence (and possibly his own test batch), hauling two jugs and a box labelled "***TSIPOURO – BATCH*** #3 – use gloves".

"You've planned an unlicensed event with unregulated alcohol and unverified entertainment?" Alex asked, arms folded, eyebrow raised.

"Yes," said Dimitri proudly.

"You're an idiot."

"Yes," he agreed again, still smiling.

The Lemon *Tsipouro* Experiment had fermented, quite literally, somewhere between Dimitri's cellar and his imagination.

"I call it *Tsipouro Lemoníko*," he announced, while pouring an alarming amount into a used jam jar. "It's local. It's organic. It's slightly medicinal."

It was also luminous.

The lemons, of course, came from the grove. He claimed their unique microclimate – "mid-mountain humidity, west-facing leaves, exposure to philosophical debates" – infused the spirit with "ethereal properties". Alex said it tasted like varnish.

But Dimitri, undeterred by common sense or biology, insisted it was ready for the public.

"*Tsipouro* Night," he declared, "will debut my greatest creation!"

"How many batches have you made?" I asked.

"Three," he said proudly. "The first two dissolved a spoon. This one only dulled it."

Alex, ever the optimist, placed a fire extinguisher behind the bar.

Claude decorated the bar with a flickering candle.

The menu read:

- *Tsipouro* Classic
- *Tsipouro* Lemon Grove (now with actual lemon!)
- *Tsipouro* Experimental
- No Refunds, No Questions, No Blame

By the time the villagers arrived that evening, the "Lemon Grove Special" had been chalked onto the menu board in a style that suggested intoxication had preceded the writing. Claude pronounced it "a sensory contradiction, like drinking nostalgia and fear".

Still, people ordered it. Because it was new. Because it was local. Because Dimitri was watching and he looked *so* hopeful.

The first sip caused silence.

The second caused coughing.

Then, from one brave soul at the back, a cry of "I can feel colours!"

From that point, it was out of our hands.

By sundown, more people had arrived.

Lots of them.

Word spread like all good things do in a Greek village: on the wind, via a cousin, and shouted from the bakery queue.

The first few chairs filled quickly with those expecting a performance. They were not disappointed, although it wasn't quite what they had been expecting.

The crowd gathered cautiously. A local doctor taped a note to the toilet door in Greek, English, and braille: "*In case of sudden blindness, blink slowly and whisper a prayer to Saint Nicholas.*"

The first round went surprisingly well. The second, less so.

By round three, Maria was speaking fluent Italian. She doesn't speak Italian. Claude was explaining quantum physics to Katerina the goat. George declared himself the rightful heir to the cheese dynasty. And Father Evangelos had quietly blessed the *tsipouro* jug, then watered a plant with it.

Kostas, a friend of Claude's, climbed the pergola, shouted "Socrates lives!", slipped, recovered, and began playing *bouzouki* while dangling by one leg. He insisted this was a new performance art movement called "existential acrobatics.".

Dimitri, meanwhile, performed a dance with an umbrella and shouted "I am Dionysus!" before knocking over a flowerpot and blaming the lemon grove spirits.

Alex leaned in towards me and whispered, "I will kill him."

"Later," I said. "He's still pouring."

And then it got weird. At some point, possibly after the fourth "experimental" shot, the night spiralled.

Someone released a chicken. It may have been symbolic.

Claude tried to do mime. Dimitri mistook it for a fight and tried to referee.

Spiros stood and proclaimed, solemnly, "This is why we don't join the European Union twice." No one was sure what he meant, but they applauded anyway.

Theodora threw *spanakopita* at a man who asked if the feta was vegan. It was not. A German woman claimed to see time bend. A French man claimed to bend it back. They later married.

At some point, the goat wandered off, and returned with friends.

The morning after, no one remembered going home.

Three chairs were missing. One had ended up in the lemon grove, engraved with a quote that read, "Drink, therefore I am."

Dimitri showed up around ten, nursing a black coffee and wearing someone else's shirt.

"I think it went well," he said.

"You caused two marriage proposals, an outbreak of prophecies, and a broken bench," I replied.

He nodded. "Better than last time."

Maria banned the event.

Eleni demanded legal documentation, a sobriety test, and an emergency goat containment strategy.

Alex made Dimitri swear never to repeat it.

And yet…

The posters stayed up, curling gently on doorposts and bus stops. People talked. The doctor discreetly ordered more bandages. And when Claude suggested introducing a wine-and-philosophy night, no one said no.

Because somehow, *Tsipouro* Night had already become a tradition.

Not scheduled. Not sanctioned. But sacred, in the way only madness, laughter, and *tsipouro* can be.

And as I watched Dimitri try to milk a lemon, "for next week's batch", I thought: this is not what we planned.

It's better.

CHAPTER TWENTY

MARY OF THE PLATES
OR "THE REASON HALF THE VILLAGE SUDDENLY NEEDED MORE BREAD"

In every Greek village, there's someone people speak of in slightly hushed tones. Not because of scandal. Not because of secrets. But because when they walk into a room, things… change.

In our village, that person was Mary.

Mary was Theodora's daughter, and George's too, though you'd be forgiven for forgetting that. George was the father, yes, he confirmed this himself once after a long ouzo and a pointed reminder. But Mary's aura, her voice, her presence, all bore the unmistakable imprint of her mother's eyebrows.

She was beauty bottled in motion. Blond curls, swift feet, and eyes that could disarm a minister or cause a grown man to trip over his own sandals while pretending to look for the loo.

She moved through Zorba's taverna like she owned the breeze. Graceful, quick, untouchable. Plates balanced on one arm, glasses refilled with a wink, arguments between tables resolved with a single raised eyebrow.

And the tourists fell hard.

Especially the ones who thought flirting in bad Greek was exotic. Mary smiled politely, then delivered their wine with the same energy one reserves for mildly inconvenient furniture.

She was beloved: by the old men who remembered her as a mischievous child; by the young men who now tried (and failed) to impress her; by the priest, who once called her "a saint in sandals"; by Katerina the goat, who followed her everywhere and once ate her apron.

"She needs a husband," Theodora muttered regularly. "A man! A future! A child who doesn't lick everything!"

George never commented. He just polished cheese knives and shook his head quietly when the topic arose.

"She has Claude," I offered once, half-joking.

"Claude is French," she snapped. "That barely counts."

It's worth noting here that Claude and Mary are not a couple, though many in the village seem determined to pretend otherwise. They like each other, yes. Genuinely. But in the way a fox and a firework might enjoy a shared sunset: beautiful, unpredictable, and best enjoyed at a safe distance.

Claude, ever poetic, once said he admired her "spirit, fire, and refusal to tolerate fools". Mary, for her part, tolerated Claude because he was fluent in flattery and surprisingly useful at carrying chairs.

They lived in the same house, technically. Claude occupied the small studio flat above the bakery Mary inherited from her grandmother. Rent was never discussed, though Claude once tried to pay her in vintage wine and badly framed poems. She declined.

The truth is, Mary was the most eligible and least interested woman in North Evia. She refused proposals like other people refused second helpings – politely, firmly, and almost daily. And she seemed perfectly happy doing so.

Over the years, the village had produced many suitors. Fishermen. Bakers. One very confident accountant with sandals and a spreadsheet. They all tried.

And they all failed.

Mary would listen politely. She'd smile, pour the wine, tilt her head like she was interested. Then, with the precision of a well-sharpened knife used only for special occasions, she'd cut them down to size. Not cruelly, but elegantly. Two sentences, maybe three, delivered so gently that the poor soul would walk away unsure whether he'd been rejected or shortlisted for sainthood.

Once, over dinner, Theodora tried again.

"You need a husband," she said, folding grape leaves like she was rolling up arguments.

"I don't need another boss," Mary replied, without looking up. "I already run a kitchen, a floor, a full taverna, and occasionally, my mother. If I find someone who can mop without turning it into a lecture about tradition, we'll talk."

"But children?" Theodora began, eyes already misting with hypothetical baptisms.

Mary raised a hand. "Let me be clear. I love children. I just don't want to marry one. And so far, that's all that's been on offer."

George, sitting quietly with his cheese, muttered something supportive, possibly by accident.

That was the end of that.

Mary worked harder than anyone. She was the first to arrive and the last to leave. She knew which tourist was allergic to shellfish, which table always wanted bread twice, and which wine bottle had a cork that required spiritual intervention.

She didn't complain. Much. She didn't gossip. Often. And she didn't accept help unless it was from Katerina, who once stood watch while Mary tied her shoelace mid-service.

She had no time for fools, liars, or anyone who asked if feta came from cows.

She loved her mother fiercely and told her so by rolling her eyes and adding more oregano to the moussaka.

She loved George too but expressed it by fixing things when he wasn't looking.

Some say Mary once carried seven plates, two wine jugs, and a tourist's crying baby, all at once.

Some say she once made a group of Swedish backpackers cry tears of joy with just a nod and a plate of *dolmades*.

Some say she once slapped a wasp to death with a menu mid-order without breaking eye contact.

All of it might be true.

And if not, it should be.

Theodora still prays for a wedding. She's even hinted at sending applications to a matchmaking show in Athens.

"Just imagine," she said once, "you could be on TV! Like feta: famous but still authentic."

Mary just snorted. "If I want drama, I'll start charging Claude rent."

And maybe one day she will marry. Maybe she won't.

But either way, the village agrees on one thing: Mary doesn't need rescuing.

She's not a princess.

She's the one who rescues others.

As for us, we just try to stay out of her way. Offer coffee when she needs it. Tell tourists to order clearly. And thank the gods, the sea, and possibly the goat, that we live in a village with someone like Mary.

    The daughter of Theodora.

    The grace of the taverna.

    The one woman in Greece who could silence a room with a glance and serve baklava five seconds later without spilling a crumb. She's still unmarried. She's still majestic.

    And she's absolutely, gloriously, part of the family.

CHAPTER TWENTY-ONE

The Man from the Municipality (and the Goat)

The letter arrived folded in quarters, hand-delivered by a man in mirrored sunglasses who neither smiled nor introduced himself. He simply asked for "the responsible party", handed over the envelope, and vanished in a puff of petrol fumes and bureaucratic menace, narrowly avoiding Katerina, who tried to eat his trouser leg as a farewell gesture.

Alex opened it with a butter knife and a glare.

"Well?" I asked, already bracing for the word demolition.

"It's from the forestry department," she said, scanning it twice. "They're sending someone to 'inspect the land directly adjacent to the licensed premises."

We both looked out the window. At the lemon grove. At Dimitri's buzzing bee crates, Claude's lopsided folding table, George's unofficial compost pile, and Maria who, at that precise moment, was leading a pair of English tourists into the grove while explaining its "deep spiritual significance to the region".

And, naturally, at Katerina, balanced on the roof of a storage shed, chewing a laminated menu and staring directly into our souls.

"They're coming tomorrow," Alex said, exhaling.

Of course they were. News of the inspection spread faster than the last time someone's donkey went missing and was found asleep in the mayor's vegetable patch.

Maria blamed Eleni. Eleni blamed Claude. Claude blamed European agricultural overregulation and began rehearsing a monologue about cultural preservation that included the words "citron sovereignty".

Dimitri began moving his hives "somewhere more discreet", which in Dimitri's world meant under the kitchen porch. Theodora tried to uproot her oregano garden and, in doing so, accidentally destroyed George's compost experiment. George took it personally and threatened to withhold cheese from everyone but the priest.

Even Spiros muttered, "Here we go again," which confused everyone, since no one could remember it happening the first time.

And Katerina, sensing the rising tension, became unhelpfully visible, dragging a folding chair into the grove, attempting to mount the compost bin, and licking the side mirror of a parked scooter.

Alex, somehow, remained calm. "We'll show them it's a village initiative," she said.

"What if they ask for permits?"

"We smile. We offer coffee. We point at the sea."

I nodded. "Classic defence."

He arrived in a municipal car that looked recently borrowed and permanently on the verge of mechanical disintegration. The man was tall, dry-looking, and carried a clipboard like it had been personally blessed by bureaucracy itself. He introduced himself as Mr Fotopoulos. No first name.

We led him around the grove like guilty tour guides. He walked slowly, taking notes, occasionally pausing to examine something – a tree trunk, a lemon, a patch of bare earth – with the solemnity of someone investigating mild heresy.

Maria tried to distract him with a slice of cake. It worked… briefly. Then he crouched beside a stone near the old fence, poked it with a biro, and frowned. "Has anyone built anything recently?" he asked.

"No!" we all said in unison, which is exactly what people say when they have absolutely built something recently. He sniffed the air. Dimitri's bees buzzed ominously.

Then Katerina trotted up and headbutted his clipboard.

He blinked. She blinked. They reached a silent understanding, and she wandered off, having made her point.

Eventually, he straightened, checked something off his clipboard, and said, "You'll receive a follow-up in writing. Within sixty days."

Then he got back into the car, waved with two fingers, and drove off in a cloud of lemon-scented dust and faint goat hair.

We waited a full minute before anyone spoke.

"He definitely knows," Eleni said.

"Knows what?" asked George.

"That we don't know what we're doing."

"He didn't stop us," Alex said calmly. "He just... observed."

"Maybe he's seen worse," I offered.

Maria scoffed. "Not unless he's been to Chalkida."

The grove held its breath. We knew it would likely be sixty days before we heard anything official, he'd said so himself, but still, part of us expected a sudden return. A missing signature. A reinspection. A penalty for using oregano without a licence.

But by sundown, nothing had happened. No notices. No fines. No inspectors climbing back over the fence waving forgotten forms.

We were exhausted. And slightly haunted.

Even Katerina, for once, was quiet, curled under a lemon tree, chewing on what might have once been the corner of a zoning map. But the grove felt different. Quieter. As if it, too, was waiting.

"Do you think they'll take it away from us?" I asked Alex that evening as we stood beneath one of the older trees, the last lemons catching the golden light.

She shook her head. "They won't," she said.

"And if they do?"

She smiled, picking a lemon from a low branch and holding it like something sacred.

"Then we'll plant another one. Somewhere else. And call it the same name."

Katerina bleated softly from the shadows. We took it as agreement.

CHAPTER TWENTY-TWO

DIPLOMACY IN HOOVES

True to his word, Zorba turned up exactly one month after we'd reopened, sat at the bar, and muttered, "Fine. I'll buy the first round."

He then proceeded to "forget his wallet" and paid in advice, which, by village standards, counted as currency. We accepted it. Barely.

Mana was in her usual spot. Perched near the kitchen door, olive bowl in hand, apron unstained (through sheer will), and gaze sharp enough to slice courgettes. Katerina lay nearby in the shade of the olive press, one leg tucked, one ear twitching, chewing something that might once have been part of a brochure.

A tourist family had arrived. German, polite, curious, the kind who asked questions like, "Is this oregano wild, or farmed?" and referred to *tsipouro* as "agricultural gin". They were lovely. Until the boy, maybe eight, maybe mildly possessed, wandered over to Katerina holding out a biscuit and shouted, "Shake!"

Mana glanced up. Katerina stared at the biscuit. The child wiggled it. "Shake!"

Katerina, in a rare moment of restraint, did not immediately eat the child. Instead, she looked to Mana.

And I swear this happened. Mana nodded. Slowly. Like Zeus granting a thunderbolt.

Then she said, "*Apoklisi to dexi.*" (Offer your right.)

And the goat lifted her hoof. It wasn't elegant, nor was it immediate, but unmistakably she raised it, just enough to slap the child's hand and knock the biscuit to the floor.

The taverna gasped. The child giggled. Katerina ate the biscuit. Mana returned to her olives like nothing had happened.

From that moment, it became a ritual. Tourists lined up with crackers, breadcrumbs, one man tried a fig. Mana, unimpressed, watched each interaction with the weary patience of a monarch overseeing a particularly ridiculous court.

Claude tried to teach Katerina to curtsy. She responded by stealing his scarf and peeing in his shoe.

Theodora declared the whole thing a distraction. "The girl needs discipline," she said. "And I'm not sure which girl I mean."

Father Evangelos arrived to observe and possibly exorcise, but left after Katerina gave him a gentle headbutt and affectionately chewed a corner of his cassock.

George said nothing but was later seen trying to teach a chicken to bow.

I watched Mana hold court over her one-hoofed pupil, handing out olives and occasional instructions. "You see?" she said once, gesturing to the goat. "Everyone needs to earn their keep."

"But you're not teaching her tricks," I said. "You're teaching her diplomacy."

Mana shrugged. "Same thing in this village."

And so the legend grew: the goat who could shake hands. Peace broker. Biscuit thief. Symbol of cross-species understanding.

Zorba, of course, just grunted and muttered, "As long as she doesn't serve drinks, I don't care."

Katerina shook hands with three more tourists that day. Then she climbed onto a table and fell asleep in a salad bowl. A true diplomat knows when to withdraw.

CHAPTER TWENTY-THREE

The Letter

It arrived, as all ominous letters in Greece do, at the exact moment we'd stopped worrying about it.

It was early. Three weeks after the lemon grove inspection, on a sleepy Thursday morning, long after Claude had gone back to experimenting with "olive oil tasting notes", and Maria had resumed selling lemon liqueur "for medicinal purposes".

Spiros was napping. The sun was already too high. And then the postman's moped sputtered into view, trailing dust and bad news.

"Letter for the taverna," he said, handing over a thick official envelope that crackled with threat. "Feels like regulations."

Alex held it like a bomb that needed defusing with cutlery. Eleni appeared from nowhere. "Do you want me to read it?" she offered, already holding a pair of bifocals and a biro.

"I've got it," Alex said, slicing it open with the confidence of a woman who had argued successfully with both the tax office and Katerina in the same week.

We gathered around the bar. Claude lit a candle "for mood". Maria poured wine "for nerves". Dimitri sharpened a stick "just in case".

Alex unfolded the letter.

It began with six lines of department names, two reference numbers, and an accusation of "non-compliant use of naturally occurring semi-cultivated terrain adjacent to a semi-commercial zone".

We braced. Then came the conclusion:

"After visual and environmental assessment, no immediate action is required, provided that: no additional permanent structures are erected without authorisation, no trees are removed, no imported livestock is introduced, especially goats (see subsection 4B), and community use remains 'informal and non-exclusive' in nature."

There was a pause.

"Wait," I said. "Is that... permission?"

Eleni adjusted her glasses. "That's a yes."

"A Greek yes," Alex clarified. "Not so much permission, more the quiet agreement that no one's going to stop you."

Claude wept quietly into his wine. Dimitri slapped the bar. Maria declared she would be launching a grove-themed yoga class immediately.

Alex flipped the letter over. There, handwritten in biro, was a note from the inspector himself:

"This grove is clearly loved. Continue to love it responsibly."

And beneath that:

"Fotopoulos. Forestry Division.

(P.S. The cake was very good.)"

That night, we held an impromptu dinner under the trees. No music, just conversation, candlelight, and a slight breeze that made the lemons sway like lanterns.

Alex raised her glass.

"To the grove," she said.

"To bureaucracy that looks the other way," added Eleni.

"To Fotopoulos," said Maria, already sketching his face for future jam labels.

Even Spiros toasted, with lemonade. And I looked around at our crooked tables, at Claude fussing with fairy lights, at Theodora guarding her oregano like sacred scripture, and I thought, it's ours. Not because a letter said so. But because we never stopped believing it already was.

CHAPTER TWENTY-FOUR

VASSILIKI
THE BAKER FROM HEAVEN

Every village has someone who feeds the body and, by some quiet miracle, also manages to feed the soul. In Telios, that person is Vassiliki.

Her bakery smells like forgiveness. Like a fresh start. Like all the mistakes you've made in your life could be absolved with a warm *koulouri* and a nod from her behind the counter.

She is not a large woman, nor loud, nor flashy. But she possesses the quiet command of someone who has mastered heat, time, and the delicate relationship between yeast and weather. When Vassiliki enters a room, people instinctively shift to make space for her. Not out of fear; out of reverence. And possibly out of self-preservation, in case she's holding a tray of *bougatsa*.

She was not born in the village. This was a scandal at first.

She arrived twenty years ago from a town no one could pronounce properly, wearing black from head to toe and a facial expression that suggested she'd already assessed everyone's character and wasn't wildly impressed.

But then, then she started baking.

The first batch was simple: bread. Crusty, blistered loaves that arrived still singing from the oven. The second was *koulouria*, hot and sesame-slicked, the kind that makes grown men weep. And by the time she introduced her *galaktoboureko*, the village council was convening to see if they could grant her honorary native status.

Even Maria, who trusts no one and suspects most outsiders of secret agendas, declared, "She's clearly sent by God. Or at least one of the more competent saints."

It helps that Vassiliki never tried to impress anyone. She didn't host village dinners or hand out samples. She simply opened her doors every morning before dawn and let the smell do the talking.

Her pastries became the stuff of legend.

People came from neighbouring villages, and once, a tourist from Denmark burst into tears after biting into one of her *tiropitas.* "It tastes like something my grandmother would have made," she sobbed. "If my grandmother had been Greek. And knew how to cook."

Children worship her. Grown men flirt with her and are instantly, politely ignored. The mayor once asked for her recipe for walnut cake. She looked at him for five seconds, then turned back to her dough. The conversation was over.

She doesn't write anything down. All her recipes are memorised, passed down through instinct, mood, and muscle. When asked, she shrugs. "You feel when it's ready," she says. "The dough tells you. If it's grumpy, leave it alone."

Once, she agreed to let someone help. A young man from Athens, doing a "culinary internship". He lasted three days. On the fourth, he tried to tell her how to improve her dough. He was never seen again.

Vassiliki doesn't gossip. She absorbs. She listens from behind her counter, as villagers collect their daily loaves and unburden themselves. She hears things long before they reach Maria's radar, but unlike Maria, she doesn't repeat them. She simply nods, offers a biscuit, and lets the warmth do its work.

And she never judges. Not when someone forgets to pay. Not when someone pays in coins and apologies. Not when someone stumbles in after a long night and asks, quietly, for "whatever's warm and forgiving".

She's seen heartbreaks, weddings, pregnancies (announced and otherwise), fallouts, reconciliations, and one spontaneous poetry reading by Claude that lasted twenty-six unbearable minutes. Through it all, she kept kneading, folding, proofing, baking. As if she were holding the village together one roll at a time.

She lives alone. Not lonely: alone. Her little house next to the bakery is filled with herbs, recipe books in at least four languages, and a cat named Apollo who hates everyone except her. No one knows her full story. There are whispers, of course. A lost love. A difficult past. A reason she left where she came from. But Vassiliki never confirms or denies anything. She simply turns on the oven and lets the truth rise where it needs to.

She attends church on feast days but always slips out before the crowd. She leaves her name on the list for prayers but never prays out loud. And every so often, on quiet weekday mornings, you can find her in the back pew, eyes closed, hands still dusted with flour, as if offering something up that words can't reach.

Once, during a power cut, the whole village panicked. Shops closed. Chaos reigned. But Vassiliki lit the old wood stove she said she kept "just in case" and kept baking.

By afternoon, the square smelled like a warm hug wrapped in cinnamon.

She handed out bread to anyone who passed by. No charge. No fuss.

When the lights came back, someone asked how she managed it.

She shrugged. "The dough was ready. What was I going to do – let it go to waste?"

Zorba's Parthenon - A Taverna by the Sea

Vassiliki never asks for thanks.

But we thank her anyway. In smiles. In clean plates. In quiet reverence as we take that first bite.

She may not be from here by birth. But she belongs to Telios more than the olives, the sea, or the grudges we never let go of. She is our baker. Our soft place. Our unspoken comfort.

Vassiliki – blessed be her *bougatsa*. And may her hands never grow tired.

CHAPTER TWENTY-FIVE

Don't Mess with the Bench

Some villages have monuments. Ours had a bench.

Spiros's bench. Ancient. Unyielding. Entirely immovable, both physically and emotionally. It sat just beneath the olive tree at the far corner of the taverna's front, overlooking the sea like it was waiting for the Persian navy to try again. It was more than wood and rusted bolts. It was history. It was habit. It was Spiros's. And, therefore, it was not to be touched.

Until Eleni touched it.

It began with laminated paper, as so many village feuds do. Eleni had prepared a proposal: "Optimisation of Circulation and

Emergency Pathways", complete with diagrams, arrows, and a bright red circle around – you guessed it – the bench.

"The whole patio bottlenecks right here," she said, pointing with her pen like a general at war. "This bench is a hazard."

"To whom?" asked Alex, though she already regretted asking.

"To progress," Eleni snapped. Maria gasped. Not dramatically. Religiously.

Dimitri raised a hand. "May I ask a clarifying question?"

"No, Dimitri," said Eleni. "This bench," she said, loud enough to be heard in two postcodes, "is in the way. It needs to go."

Spiros stood. Slowly. Like a storm brewing from a clear sky.

"The only thing in the way is bureaucracy," he said, pointing a finger that had likely pointed at invading tanks.

Eleni crossed her arms. "This is not personal."

"Everything with you is personal."

"It's municipal!"

"Exactly."

Because Eleni and Spiros had history. The village had always tried to stay neutral, but neutrality is hard when you remember funerals.

Before Spiros became the immovable presence on the bench, part sculpture, part sentry, part public inconvenience, he had had a job. A real one. He ran the village cemetery. Not officially, of course. There was no badge, no uniform. But for years,

Spiros was the gravedigger, the weed remover, the emergency cross-straightener, and the seasonal florist, depending on mood and rainfall. He knew every stone by name, every crack in the churchyard path, and every story buried beneath it – including a few that had never made it to confession.

Sometimes he'd tend the graves with quiet reverence, clearing weeds, planting geraniums, adjusting crooked photos like they were family. Other times, he'd disappear for a week and claim the souls had asked for privacy.

If a cross toppled in a storm, Spiros would be there the next day, hammer in one hand, cigarette in the other, muttering about "shoddy modern materials" and "the dignity of oak". He took his duties seriously. Even if no one had officially given them to him.

Some said he did it out of respect. Others said he liked the peace and quiet. Maria claimed he once slept in the crypt "for clarity of thought", though no one had the courage to ask him directly.

Either way, by the time he retired, or possibly just stopped going, the cemetery had never looked more haphazardly loved. And now, he brought that same level of silent custodianship to his bench. Different plot. Same philosophy. Sit long enough, smoke slowly enough, and everything else will sort itself out.

Eventually.

"You think I forgot?" Eleni now hissed across the taverna courtyard, slamming a hand down on the table. "You let dandelions grow over my husband's resting place!"

"He was underground," Spiros shot back. "He didn't need the view!"

A gasp rippled through the tables like a breeze through scandal.

Father Evangelos crossed himself.

Dimitri whispered, "Again?" and passed around grilled sardines like communion wafers for the dismayed.

Maria, sensing opportunity, began narrating the altercation to three confused Danish tourists in real time: "And now, she brings up the grave. Yes, again. It's tradition."

And there it was. The feud, rekindled. Smouldering with the embers of something that had once involved a community council vote, a broken trellis, and a water bill from 1994.

But as in all great village dramas, people chose sides before fully understanding the argument.

Maria declared herself neutral but began keeping an official score on the bakery blackboard:

BENCH SITUATION:
SPIROS 1 – ELENI 0 – CHAOS 7

Claude insisted the bench had "existential implications" and should be preserved as a place of "philosophical pause". He began hosting sunset meditations beside it, which only annoyed everyone further.

Theodora threatened to hit the next person who mentioned "urban planning" with a rolling pin.

George, caught in the middle, made cheese and pretended he was deaf.

Dimitri built a second bench out of two crates, three fishing rods, and a traffic cone, declaring it "the bench of the future". It collapsed within twelve minutes.

Things were escalating. The next day, Eleni arrived with a tape measure and her cousin, who claimed to be "in traffic engineering". He turned out to be a retired dentist, but that didn't stop him from suggesting the bench violated "seating load regulations".

Spiros, in turn, chained himself to the bench.

Literally.

"It's symbolic," he said, sipping *tsipouro* through a straw.

Alex tried to mediate. "Let's all take a breath."

"He's chained to the furniture!" Eleni shouted.

"At least he's not carrying a clipboard," muttered Theodora.

Katerina the goat arrived midway through the shouting, sniffed the bench, and promptly climbed onto it, chewing Eleni's laminated plan with great satisfaction.

"Even the goat agrees with me!" Eleni yelled.

"She's unbiased," said Dimitri. "She chews everyone's paperwork."

Father Evangelos appeared that evening. He wasn't summoned, he just sensed he was needed, the way wise men do.

He stood between the two combatants, looked at the bench, looked at the goat, then removed his glasses and began to clean them, which, in our village, is the liturgical equivalent of slamming a gavel.

"This bench," he said, finally, "is older than half the buildings here."

"Exactly," said Eleni. "It's obsolete."

"And that is why it stays."

Spiros grunted in triumph.

"But," the priest continued, "perhaps it could be... polished. And not used to store sardine tins."

Spiros nodded solemnly.

"And Eleni... perhaps a new pathway could be created, around it. Progress, as you say, requires imagination."

Eleni looked like she'd bitten a lemon. Then she nodded, just once.

Maria updated the board the next morning:

BENCH SITUATION:
SPIROS 1 – ELENI 1 – GOAT WINS

Spiros remains on the bench. No longer chained, but watchful.

Eleni now walks around it, pointedly, every day.

Claude erected a small wooden sign that reads: "Historical

Artefact: Do Not Debate."

Dimitri's replacement bench was found floating in the harbour.

George is still pretending he's deaf.

Katerina sleeps under the bench now, curled in the shade, occasionally glaring at Eleni.

A new tradition, it seems. It's also a reminder, as always, that in our village, no decision is too small to divide the population, especially when it involves somewhere to sit.

INTERLUDE

PART 2

ON LEARNING TO BE GREEK
WHAT I'VE LEARNED

There are things I've learned since becoming an honorary Greek. For example:

- Ask for seconds, and you'll get thirds. Refuse, and they'll worry you're dying. There is no winning, only eating.

- Never ask what time something starts. It begins when it begins, which is either twenty minutes ago or sometime next Tuesday.

- Never, under any circumstances, suggest that someone's olive oil tastes the same as someone else's. It will always end in tears. That way lies war.

What I Still Can't Quite Master

I have been Greek now, or at least *Greek-adjacent*, for many years. I married into the madness. I've lived the festivals, survived the bureaucracy, and once made it through a 14-course Easter dinner without blacking out. And yet, there are still things I can't quite manage.

I will never understand how Greek drivers interpret red lights as "mild suggestions".

I will never fully grasp the mystery of the Greek post office, where packages disappear into myth and occasionally reappear smelling of oregano.

And I will never master the secret art of *Greek time*. If someone tells you they'll meet you at 6 p.m., they might mean 7. They might mean tomorrow. They might already be there, having changed their mind, but forgotten to tell you. You'll never know until they appear, or don't.

Things I Thought I Understood (But Didn't)

Language. I thought I spoke passable Greek. I passed tests. I had halting conversations with waiters and taxi drivers. Then I met Maria's cousin from the next village who spoke so fast I thought he was naming gods.

Hospitality. I thought I knew how to be polite. Then I turned down a third slice of cake and was treated as if I'd insulted the ancestors.

Volume. I thought I knew what a "loud conversation" was. Then I heard Theodora and Mary debate the best spinach pie recipe. From three streets away.

What I've Really Learned

Despite my failings, here's what I do know now:

Greek life is not about control. It's about adaptation. If the butcher's is closed, you ask his cousin. If the bus doesn't come, you get a ride from someone who might be your neighbour or might be the mayor. Either way, you'll arrive eventually, probably with a melon.

Greek love is not quiet. It's loud. It's messy. It's unapologetic. And it's never conditional.

Greek time is not late. It's based on *readiness*. Emotionally. Logistically. Existentially.

And Greek community is not chosen. *It chooses you.* Sometimes through a plate of *moussaka*. Sometimes by dragging you into a local election you didn't know existed. But once you're in, you're in.

Alex says I'm more Greek than I realise. Which is lovely, until I forget the name of a relative or confuse feta with *anthotyro* and get scolded like a stray cat.

But I've learned that being Greek isn't about being born here. It's about showing up. It's about caring enough to argue. It's about offering a seat, even if there's no chair. It's about feeding someone, and then asking if they're trying to starve themselves to death because they didn't finish the fifth plate.

It's about presence.

And after all these years, I may never master Greek grammar, I may never win an argument with a *yiayia*, but I've learned to show up. And I've learned to stay.

And in Greece, that's more than enough.

CHAPTER TWENTY-SIX

THE GROVE DIVIDE

One day, Maria made a batch of lemon liqueur. Recycled wine bottles, hand-written labels that read "From the Heart of the Grove", and a neat little sign that said "Two euros a glass – all proceeds to grove maintenance."

No one knew what "grove maintenance" actually involved, but it sounded wholesome, and people clapped. Eleni got misty-eyed. Claude offered to write a poem for the label.

The very next morning, Dimitri arrived early – too early – carrying a single bottle of his own. He said nothing. He just placed it next to Maria's display with the solemnity of someone laying down a gauntlet.

His bottle was unlabelled. Wax-sealed. Slightly sticky.

He called it *Tsipouro Lemonaki*, and when asked about ingredients, offered only a wink and the phrase "for medicinal purposes".

It wasn't new. It was the same concoction he'd trialled during the infamous *Tsipouro* Night that ended with Claude asleep in the oregano and Spiros declaring his intention to marry a squid. But this time, it was personal.

Maria sniffed the bottle but said nothing.

Dimitri sat at his usual table, poured a small measure, and sipped.

War had begun.

Silent. Citrus-scented. And almost certainly illegal.

By lunchtime, Claude had announced a plan to host a monthly *Salon du Citron* in the grove, featuring poetry, philosophical debates, and what he described as "seasonal tartlets".

And by sunset, Theodora had issued an informal ban on using "her oregano", grown in the grove, for anything involving tartlets.

That was the moment we realised: the grove wasn't just a grove any more.

It was becoming *valuable*.

And that, in a Greek village, is where things get complicated.

There weren't meetings. There were *conversations*. Mostly at tables, usually with wine, and often with a dramatic gesture towards the trees.

Some believed the grove should be a shared space. "It belongs to the village," they said, "to the people who breathe it, walk it, *remember* it."

Others saw opportunity.

Eleni, now in possession of a branded apron and something resembling a business plan, began referring to the grove as "Phase One". She'd sourced jars for lemon marmalade, ordered packaging from Athens, and was already scouting for a website developer with "rustic digital sensibility".

Maria was collecting testimonials. "Tourists love authenticity," she said. "If they believe this grove is special, it *is* special."

George mostly wanted to be left alone with his compost, which was now being referred to by Maria as "organic enhancement". He didn't understand it, but he liked the sound of it.

And Spiros just kept showing up, sitting under the same tree, smoking in contemplative silence. When asked his opinion, he'd shrug and say, "Lemons grow where the land is patient. People are rarely as patient as the land."

Nobody quite knew what that meant. But everyone nodded, as if they did.

While the rest of us danced around ownership, branding, and invisible boundaries, Alex had carried on preparing. Without any fuss, she had been pulling weeds, fixing the broken gate, sweeping the little path where the fig tree overhung, and hanging a string of lights between two trees. Not because she had a plan, but because it made the space beautiful.

"What are you doing?" I asked one evening, as she tied a final knot in the faded ribbon around the lemon tree and stepped back.

"Reminding it that it's loved," she said. "That's how you keep something yours. Not by claiming it, but by showing up for it."

She wasn't trying to win the grove. She was trying not to lose what it had already become.

Of course, it wouldn't be a Greek village without a rumour, and this one arrived wrapped in whispers and carried on the breeze.

A cousin of a friend of the mayor's second wife had allegedly spoken to someone at the municipality. They'd heard that "development interest" had been shown in the area.

Not a hotel, necessarily. But maybe… a wellness centre. That word, "wellness", dropped into the village like a foreign coin.

Claude was delighted. Maria looked thoughtful. Dimitri spat into the dust. I looked at Alex, who was watching the lemon trees sway gently in the evening light. I could see her jaw tighten. Just a little.

The grove was no longer quiet. People began referring to it as "THE GROVE", capitalised and reverent. Children were told not to run through it. The mayor's secretary came to "see how it was looking".

Someone posted a photograph of it online. The caption read: "Hidden gem of North Evia. Magical lemon grove, steps from the sea."

Alex printed the photo, then folded it in half and used it as a coaster.

We were still serving grilled sardines and refilling wine glasses, but the grove, once wild and half-forgotten, was now something else. Something everyone had noticed. And soon, something someone would want to own.

CHAPTER TWENTY-SEVEN

INFLUENCE THIS

She introduced herself as Calliope Wanderlust. Though her passport almost certainly still said Sandra Higgins from Milton Keynes.

She arrived wearing floaty trousers, a wide-brimmed hat capable of shading three counties, and sunglasses that looked like they'd once belonged to a Bond villain.

And she was holding a very large, very expensive camera. Pointed directly at Spiros's shoes.

Claude greeted her like a minor deity who had descended from Olympus with a sponsored content deal. "She's got two hundred thousand followers," he whispered. "She's a cultural ambassador!"

"She just asked if the goat was part of the décor," Alex muttered.

Katerina, lounging in the sun with a stolen paper napkin dangling from her mouth like a cigar, blinked slowly and belched like a dignified sailor. The blogger took a photo.

She chose a table perilously close to Spiros's bench, a territorial line rarely crossed without consequence.

Spiros shifted. He sighed. Then, just loud enough for everyone and no one to hear, he muttered:

"They come for the olives. They stay for the soul. And then they open a fish spa with fish that eat feet."

No one responded. No one asked what he meant.

Partly because this was Spiros – and partly because, in Greece, there's always a chance he's referring to something that actually happened.

He picked up his *komboloi* and gave it a sharp flick, as if punctuating an ancient warning passed down through generations. We carried on pretending not to hear him, but Maria muttered, without looking up, "Last time, it was frozen yoghurt." And everyone went a little quiet.

Mary, appointed (unwillingly) as Calliope's server, approached our new guest with a notebook and the facial expression of someone preparing themselves for surgery without anaesthetic.

Calliope ordered slowly, asking questions like:

- "Is the fish locally distressed?"
- "Do the olives have a narrative arc?"
- "Is the lemon grove available for private events?"

Mary didn't blink. "Everything here is available. For the right price. Except the priest."

Claude hovered nearby, offering to read her some French poetry and something he called "ambient prose". He insisted she capture the light under the pergola "before it gets shy".

Maria offered her a spoonful of her marmalade. The blogger licked it from the spoon, closed her eyes, and murmured, "Emotionally granular."

"Is that good?" Maria asked.

"Unclear," Claude replied. "But it has potential."

She photographed everything.

The table. The sky. A fork. A slightly confused stray cat. Spiros's ancient sandals (still on his feet, still defiantly on his sacred bench). She called it "rustic realism".

When the *saganaki* arrived, golden and fizzing like a small edible volcano, she screamed, "Nobody touch that!" then spent the next twenty minutes photographing it from seventeen angles, including crouching, standing on a chair, and once, briefly, from under the table.

By the time she allowed anyone to eat it, the cheese had gone cold and Alex had developed a new facial twitch.

"She's a storyteller," Claude said, his eyes alight with the madness of untapped internet fame. "This could go viral!"

"She hasn't eaten anything," Alex hissed.

"Exactly! Art before appetite!"

Dimitri emerged with a grilled octopus and a lit cigarette in the same hand. Calliope asked if the octopus had a name. He stared at her for a beat, then said, "Yes. Stavros."

She wrote that down.

Theodora, who had been watching from the kitchen window like a hawk monitoring a mouse, stormed out holding a tray of baked lamb.

"She has not touched the *saganaki*," she snapped.

"She's composing," Claude said dreamily.

"She is *disrespecting* the cheese," Theodora growled. "It is delicate. It has a window."

"She says she's full," Mary offered.

"She hasn't *eaten anything*," Theodora barked. "Not even the parsley!"

Just as Calliope began photographing her wine glass against the backdrop of Claude playing a single, uncertain note on his accordion, Katerina made her entrance.

She trotted onto the patio like a celebrity arriving fashionably late, sniffed the blogger's designer tote bag, licked a breadstick, and then, with admirable efficiency, sneezed directly onto her sandals.

Calliope cried actual tears.

"She's perfect," she whispered. "Raw. Ancient. Slightly chewy."

She posted the photo with the caption: "Unfiltered goat energy. A metaphor for the Greek soul."

Katerina, satisfied, climbed onto a chair and fell asleep.

Later that evening, Zorba finally asked the question.

"What is... a blog?"

We all paused.

Claude launched into an explanation involving algorithms, narrative curation, and "digital experiential resonance".

Zorba held up a hand. "No. What is a blog?"

Alex sighed. "It's like gossip. But global."

Zorba grunted, poured himself a *tsipouro*, and said, "Then let the goat do the interviews."

The next morning, the post went live. A glowing, poetic, utterly bewildering review. "Zorba's: A whispering taverna where sea meets soul. The wine tastes like wisdom.

The food was not consumed but emotionally understood.

Highlights include:

- An octopus named Stavros

- Existential olives
- A goat who sees into your past lives.

The photo of Spiros's feet got 12,000 likes.

Alex stood behind the bar; arms folded. "She didn't eat a single thing," she muttered.

"She called our oregano 'gritty narrative,'" I added helpfully.

Claude, glowing, was already planning a second influencer night. "Next time," he whispered, "we let her name the octopus."

Of course... The tourists arrived. One asked to sit "in the emotional goat zone". Another wanted "the plate that speaks of generational trauma". Someone tried to pet the oregano.

Katerina began posing automatically every time a phone was raised. Maria declared herself the "Herbal Curator of Authentic Emotional Condiments".

Theodora banned smartphones within ten metres of the stove and started slamming down plates like punctuation marks.

And we served food. Smiled politely. Resisted the urge to scream when someone asked if our lemons were "socially conscious". Because at Zorba's, the food is local. The staff are slightly unstable. And the chaos? The chaos is now... online, and global.

CHAPTER TWENTY-EIGHT

The Tourist Invasion

After the blog had gone viral, suddenly, we were known, and people wanted to visit. It began, of course, with a rumour. Because in Greek villages, that's how fate sends out its invitations.

"Bus is coming," said George.

"A *bus*?" I asked.

"Full of tourists," he added darkly, as though discussing an incoming storm, or a biblical plague. "German ones."

"I'm sure they mean well," I said.

George gave me a look normally reserved for people who

bring almond-feta to a village feast.

By lunchtime, Maria had confirmed it through three sources (two cousins and a passing dog walker): a full-size coach, heading straight for Telios. Destination? Zorba's.

We were unprepared. Of course, we were always unprepared, but this was different. These weren't wanderers or foodies. These were "package people". Sun hats. Matching lanyards. Bottled water. Gluten questions.

Alex stood on the patio, arms crossed, scanning the horizon like a general waiting for the invasion. Theodora started sharpening knives. Dimitri vanished entirely.

Then we heard it: the low, whining approach of diesel-fuelled doom. The bus arrived. It parked sideways.

And twenty-eight enthusiastic, sensible-shoed tourists poured into our village like a polite flood. They were led by a guide named Petra, a cheerful woman with a clipboard, a headset, and the gaze of someone who once taught at a nursery school and never really stopped.

"We're here for an *authentic* Greek lunch," she said.

Alex smiled, the kind of smile that suggests someone is about to be fed or arrested. Possibly both.

The group settled like cats into our mismatched chairs, waving maps and fanning themselves with pamphlets. "I'd like a tuna melt," said the first tourist.

"No," said Theodora.

"I'm allergic to dairy," said another.

"You can have wine," Theodora replied.

One asked for a salad "without onions, olives, or tomatoes".

"You want a bowl," said Mary flatly.

They ordered coffee before food. Then milk before coffee. Then ice cubes. Theodora looked at me. I pretended to be busy writing a menu that did not exist.

"Is there live music?" asked a man wearing socks with sandals.

Claude perked up immediately. "I can do a performance."

"*Jazz*?" asked the man.

Claude's eyes glowed. "Camus meets Miles Davis."

"No," said Alex from the kitchen.

Claude quietly packed away his tambourine.

As the confusion peaked, Dimitri reappeared triumphantly, carrying a string of freshly caught fish like a prize fighter, and wearing an octopus around his neck. A German teenager tried to pet them. One woman gasped, "Are they... dead?"

Dimitri blinked. "Only on the outside."

Then the woman's husband tried to take a selfie with the octopus. The octopus, still slightly alive, slapped him. Twice. Applause broke out from the back table, and Spiros raised his coffee.

But we muddled through. The food arrived, slowly, defiantly, one dish at a time. No one got exactly what they ordered, but everyone got something *Greek*. Theodora refused substitutions. Claude translated badly. Maria took photos of people's plates and told them they were already "internet famous". One tourist pronounced the tzatziki "revolutionary". Another declared the chairs "a health hazard". Both were right.

By the time dessert arrived – slices of watermelon and mystery cake from Vassiliki's emergency stockpile – the mood had shifted. They were laughing. Tipsy. Taking photos with Spiros (who still wasn't sure why). Dimitri was giving a lesson in olive sorting. Claude had performed two short poems and nobody had stopped him. Even Petra the tour guide, clipboard now forgotten, danced a little near the lemon grove, mouthing along to a *bouzouki* song only she could hear.

After they left, waving, clapping, promising to leave five-star reviews for "the goat taverna", we sat in the shade, breathless.

"We survived," I said.

Alex poured a glass of wine. "Barely."

"They left happy," said Mary, sipping slowly.

Theodora grunted. "I need two days' sleep and a new ladle."

Spiros nodded sagely. "Tourists are like hiccups. You complain, then miss them when they're gone."

Claude raised a glass. "To the chaos."

CHAPTER TWENTY-NINE

Hooves and Whiskers

By now, the legend of Katerina had also travelled well beyond the village. Tourists came looking for her specifically. Some asked for a table "near the hoof-shaking goat". One couple claimed to have seen her mentioned in a blog titled "Animals of Influence". Claude considered translating her story into French and submitting it to a literary journal. Eleni, more practically, suggested we register her as a "staff mascot" to write off her food expenses. But we were just about to find out that Katerina, who we all thought was likely descended from a particularly mischievous Greek god, had a soft side.

Like any respectable Greek epic, this one involved a mysterious box, questionable timing, and a complete lack of return address.

A slightly damp, meowing cardboard box was deposited beside the taverna's bin area just after dawn. It wobbled.

Alex noticed it first. She paused, holding her mop like a sword. "Either that box contains a dying seagull or a new problem," she muttered.

I peered closer.

"Five problems," I said. "And they're all meowing."

Inside: five tiny, matted kittens. Eyes too big for their faces. Fur like abandoned sweaters. Energy somewhere between pitiful and feral. They were a mess, but cute, in that tragic way that guarantees love within seconds.

Maria appeared, phone already raised. "Oh good, something to post. Do they have names yet?"

"They don't have fleas yet," said Alex, grimly.

Eleni offered adoption forms and listed the ministries we'd need to notify. George contributed an empty feta tin, claiming it made a perfect kitten bath. Claude suggested we name them all after philosophers and began composing a haiku. Mana squinted at them and muttered something about them being "God's mousetraps with attitude". Dimitri, true to form, tried to feed them grilled sardines. They hissed. One bit him. He looked pleased.

And then she arrived: Katerina strolled around the corner

like a mother coming home late from bingo. She stopped. Stared. Snorted.

The kittens froze. So did we. There was a moment of tension, the kind you get just before Zeus hurls a thunderbolt or Theodora discovers someone used parsley in her moussaka.

Then, with the calm of a creature who's seen worse (and likely caused it), Katerina walked over to the kittens… and laid down beside them.

No one spoke. We simply watched. The kittens blinked up at her. She sniffed each one, grunted, then curled around them in a way that could only be described as… maternal.

"She's warming them," Alex whispered.

"She's claiming them," Maria whispered louder.

"She's lost her mind," said Eleni.

Katerina closed her eyes. One of the kittens began suckling on her ear. Claude gasped. "It's beautiful."

Dimitri shrugged. "Better than letting them live in the mop bucket."

From that moment, Katerina became… different. Softer. Wiser. Slightly more smug. She herded the kittens across the patio, headbutting doors open for them. She let them nap in her shadow. When a tourist's child tried to pick one up too roughly, Katerina bit his shoe and stared him down until he cried.

One kitten, the bold one with the missing tail, rode on her back. Tourists started taking photos.

Mana, of course, was not impressed. "She'll smother them," she declared.

"She hasn't yet," Alex replied.

"She's a goat, not a grandmother."

"She's doing a better job than you did when Theodora brought home that injured crow."

Mana glared. "That crow was possessed."

Still, she began appearing earlier and earlier at the taverna, sitting on her stool, watching the goat. She'd toss stale *koulourakia* near the kittens. She'd mutter threats at the cats, then sigh when they climbed into her lap.

"She's doing it wrong," she would whisper. "You don't just lie there. You clean their ears." But her voice softened. And one afternoon, when she thought no one was looking, she scratched Katerina behind the ear and said, "Good girl."

Of course there was drama. Eleni began researching tax implications for goat-led childcare. Theodora offered to make them proper food, "because goat milk and dirt is not a balanced diet."

Spiros claimed he'd seen this before, back in '61, when a sheep raised a litter of hedgehogs during a snowstorm. No one believed him, but he told the story anyway.

The kittens grew. Not gradually, but all at once, like bread dough left in the sun.

One minute they were sleepy scraps of fluff snoozing under Katerina's belly. The next, they were stalking cockroaches, stealing olives, and launching surprise attacks on tourists' shoelaces with the strategic precision of small, whiskered pirates. They climbed curtains, got stuck in wine racks, and once tried to nap in Father Evangelos's cassock during mass. (He didn't notice until the offertory.)

And Katerina? Katerina adapted. She licked their heads with weary devotion. She shared her lettuce, her sunspots, and occasionally, her more creative opinions on where to poop, such as Claude's poetry notebook, the inspector's bicycle seat, the taverna's suggestion box, the guestbook, the back of Eleni's shoe, the last page of the permit application, and once, memorably, inside an unattended handbag.

She chased off stray dogs with such explosive fury that even Dimitri called her "militarised".

One sunny morning, she marched the kittens single file down the lemon grove path, tail high, ears forward, like a goat general leading her tiny, furry army into battle.

We tried to be patient. We tried not to trip over kitten ambushes under every chair. We tried not to scream when one popped out of the flour sack at 1 a.m.

But the truth was, if Katerina had been a charming nuisance before… then Katerina plus five kittens was starting to look like an uprising.

And no one was safe. Not the guests. Not the menu. Certainly not the cheese.

They were no longer kittens, exactly. They were lanky, scruffy adolescents with too much confidence and absolutely no sense of personal boundaries. We never named them properly. Instead, we described them by their crimes:

- **Toe-Biter** – slept in shoes, pounced at ankles.
- **Souvlaki** – stole skewers, then dragged them under tables like trophies.
- **Napkin** – obsessed with paper. Entirely shredded the taverna menu stock.
- **Up** – climbed everything. Especially Claude.
- **Not Ours** – vanished for three days and returned wearing a rhinestone collar. No explanation.

Together, they were unstoppable.

Tourists adored them, at first. One couple from Denmark tried to take a selfie with Napkin. He slapped the camera out of their hands and then peed on their beach bag.

Mana threatened to throw the cats out and let them find employment elsewhere. "They're demons in fur," she said. "Sent to mock me." Still, she began leaving small bowls of milk beneath her stool, "just in case the goat forgets".

It reached a peak one Saturday night. The taverna was full. The moon was high. Katerina was napping under a table. The grill sizzled. Wine flowed. And then, like tiny hurricanes in fur coats, they struck. Toe-Biter darted into the kitchen and emerged dragging a loaf of bread. Up leapt onto a chair, then a table, then into George's arms, who, startled, dropped an entire plate of fried sardines onto Eleni's lap. Napkin shredded three serviettes in less than ten seconds. Souvlaki launched a kamikaze raid on a French tourist's starter. Not Ours licked a spoon and vanished. Theodora shouted something in Cretan that scorched the oregano.

Alex stood still for five seconds, then turned slowly to me and said, "We need to stage an intervention."

That night, beneath the lemon trees, we gathered the taverna council. Mana brought a wooden spoon. Dimitri brought *tsipouro*, "to dull the trauma". Katerina was summoned. She arrived with dignity. The kittens followed. Chaotic. Muddy. Wild-eyed.

It was Claude who finally said it.

"We need to stage an intervention."

He said it like he'd rehearsed it. Like he'd spent the night drafting poetry and the morning stepping in something soft behind the olive barrels.

Because by now, the kittens had names. Personalities. A following. One of them had its own cushion near the till and another had discovered the warmth of the *tsipouro* shelf next to one of Dimitri's glowing bottles, and refused to leave.

Maria had started leaving them saucers of milk.

Theodora had been caught, once, slicing chicken a little too generously while claiming she was "trimming the fat".

George denied everything, but we'd all seen him plaiting oregano stems into tiny collars.

We needed a decision.

Alex stood up, raising her hand like a general about to command a fleet.

"But they're family," Mary said.

That was it. That was the solution.

But even family needs rules.

So we made some:

- No kittens in the kitchen (unless Theodora wasn't looking).
- All napkins to be stored in the cupboard, behind the jars of capers, well above leap range and ego.
- Claude was forbidden from assigning astrological signs to them. Again.

Naturally, none of the rules worked.

But the kittens stayed. And the tourists started leaving tips just to photograph them asleep in the cutlery basket.

Claude was responsible for entertainment, not discipline. Mana was promoted to "Director of Feline Decency". She didn't accept the title, but she did begin brushing their fur when no one was watching.

Katerina, now known as "Mamma K" by some locals, oversaw it all. Sometimes she chased them back from trouble. Sometimes she joined them. Most nights, they all slept together beneath the biggest lemon tree.

They've grown, of course. Now they run along rooftops, watch the tourists with sly amusement, and occasionally help themselves to unattended *souvlaki*. But when one of them sneezes, Katerina checks on them. When a child cries, the cats surround them. And when the lights go out at Zorba's, they curl into her side and purr like a hymn. Goat and kittens. Madness and love.

Telios's strangest family, and maybe its most honest.

So if you visit the taverna and see a goat surrounded by cats sleeping on her back, don't ask. Just smile. And know that, in this village at least, love comes in all shapes. Some with horns. Some with claws. Some with both.

CHAPTER THIRTY

WHO OWNS THE LEMONS?

Now we had all actually agreed that the lemon grove would be used as a seating area to give the taverna more tables, we had agreed to respect people's loose claims to ownership of bits of it. The oregano patch for Theodora; the organic fertiliser from George, as long as he kept it downwind of the eating areas; Dimitri's bees, as long as they kept away from the clients.

Alex had suggested, during what was supposed to be a peaceful evening coffee, that we hang lanterns from the lemon trees instead of fairy lights.

"Gentler than bulbs," she'd said. "More flattering."

A quiet spot for late-night coffee, chess games, debates about the national football team, and the slow fading of summer wine.

"A shared space," she said, with that breezy confidence she reserves for ideas that usually turn into infrastructure projects. Everyone nodded. Slowly. Cautiously. As though they were being offered a free donkey that might bite.

Then Maria, who could find drama in a bowl of lentils, narrowed her eyes and asked, "Yes, but… whose lemons are they?"

The world stopped spinning.

Chairs stopped creaking. Coffee froze mid-sip. Even the wind, sensing trouble, took the long way around the grove.

And just like that, the grove, once a sleepy tangle of bees, brambles, and benevolent neglect, became the front line of a war no one had declared.

George was first. "They're mine," he said confidently, thumping the table with the kind of authority only available to men who've had three ouzos. "My grandfather planted them. During the Lemon Crisis of '27."

"What lemon crisis?" asked someone.

"You weren't born yet," he replied, as though that settled everything.

Not to be outdone, Spiros leaned back on his sacred bench, exhaled smoke like a prophet, and claimed the trees had sprouted naturally when his great-uncle Stavros used to graze goats there. "Lemons from nature's generosity," he said, with the calm of a man who knows no one will question him because no one wants to hear the rest of the goat story.

Dimitri said nothing, but was later spotted pushing a wheelbarrow full of lemons up the hill, whistling a tune that sounded suspiciously triumphant.

Claude, naturally, quoted Rousseau, or possibly a wine bottle, and announced that abandoned land, and by extension, lemons, belonged to "the people".

Eleni arrived with a folder of documents so old they were held together with hope and Sellotape. According to her, the lemons belonged to her great-aunt's second husband's estate, "pending clarification". She began drafting a petition for lemon access rights.

Theodora didn't care who owned the grove, just so long as nobody touched *her* lemon tree: the third one from the left, the one she insists has the best juice for liqueur, and which she has been known to talk to under her breath while stirring béchamel.

Zorba didn't say anything for three days. Then one afternoon, while peeling an orange that wasn't his, he said, "Those trees were there before any of you were born. And they'll still be here when you're all compost." Everyone took this as both a threat and a blessing.

But within a week, Maria threatened to hire her cousin's ex-boyfriend, who had once nearly passed the bar exam; Dimitri erected a ladder in the grove and harvested two buckets before anyone noticed, then denied everything while drinking lemon *tsipouro*; Eleni submitted an official land registry request, guaranteed to yield no results but excellent drama; and Claude wrote a treaty, in French, English, and his own unique dialect of poetic bureaucracy, outlining communal lemon access rights. Nobody read it, but everyone had an opinion.

Alex and I sat quietly by the gate, drinking coffee and wondering if it would be easier to declare the grove a sovereign republic, adopt a flag, and apply for EU lemon subsidies.

Of course, it was ridiculous. But underneath it all – the shouting, the accusations, the clandestine lemon collecting at dawn – was something more honest.

This wasn't about fruit. It was about feeling. Feeling connected. People weren't fighting over the lemons. They were fighting *for* them.

For the grove. For the village. For the strange, sun-soaked, tangled little piece of land that had somehow become a symbol of everything we loved about this place.

Eventually, Alex stood beneath the oldest tree, perched on an old wooden crate with her sunglasses on and her patience hanging by a thread.

"The lemons," she said, "belong to everyone. And to no one. Like the wind. Or the moon. Or the right to shout at your neighbour in the morning and bring them cake in the afternoon."

Zorba's Parthenon - A Taverna by the Sea

There was silence. A few nods. One heartfelt belch. Then Zorba raised his cup. "To the lemons," he said. And the village replied, in unison, as if rehearsed:

"To the lemons."

Chapter Thirty-One

The Fish Festival Disaster

The idea, like many Greek ideas, took shape over a slightly warm glass of wine and escalated rapidly.

"It's simple," Maria declared, waving a breadstick like a wand. "We host a Fish Festival. Everyone loves fish. Everyone loves festivals. And this" – she gestured around the taverna, which at the time was missing a ceiling fan, two chairs, and arguably structural integrity – "is our chance to shine."

Now, in theory, it wasn't a bad idea. We had the sea. We had fish. We had Dimitri.

But theory, as we were about to learn, has very little to do with Greek village reality.

Claude, naturally, took charge of branding.

He printed a banner that read:

TELIOS INTERNATIONAL AQUATIC CULINARY AND CULTURAL EXPERIENCE.

It was three metres long, bilingual, and spelled "culinary" wrong in Greek, and French. Dimitri volunteered the catch. Or rather, he *promised* he had a catch, which is not the same thing. George offered cheese tastings, despite the theme being fish.

Maria was tasked with PR, which mostly involved her loudly announcing in the bakery that Nikos's cousin's friend from Lamia worked in regional tourism, and this was "basically going to be on television".

Alex, wisely, said nothing.

Instead, she kept a running list on a napkin of all the things likely to go wrong. The napkin filled up by the second coffee.

The day before the festival, Maria ran into the taverna breathless and trembling with either excitement or caffeine.

"They're coming," she panted. "The dolphins."

"Who's coming?" I asked.

"The *dolphins!*" she repeated. "I saw three of them leaping, like *blessings!*"

I looked at Dimitri. He shrugged. "Might've been tuna."

By lunchtime, the village was buzzing. The word "dolphins" had morphed into "marine blessing" which then became "official ambassador of Poseidon". Someone started a rumour that a dolphin had kissed a Scandinavian tourist two years ago and blessed her wedding.

This, unfortunately, became the headline on Claude's redesigned banner:

"Telios Fish Festival – Where Dolphins Bless the Catch."

The day of the festival arrived. The sun was blistering. The fish, less so. Dimitri's promised catch turned out to be two squid, a confused crab, and something that may have been a shoe. Maria decorated the tables with laminated dolphin cut-outs.

Claude set up a stage made from stacked crates, a rickety plank, and borrowed fairy lights. He intended to recite sea poetry at dusk.

Stamos was in charge of power and somehow managed to plug the sound system into a faulty fuse box that sparked every time someone clapped.

The climax came at 7:04 p.m.

Just as Claude raised his arms to begin "Ode to a Sardine" (a piece he described as "haunting yet scalable"), one of the crates beneath him gave a long, splintering *crack*.

The makeshift stage shuddered.

Claude, to his credit, didn't flinch. He simply lifted one foot and attempted to turn the moment into interpretive movement.

Unfortunately, the other crate decided to join its fallen comrade.

There was a sound not unlike a snapping breadstick followed by a very small scream.

Claude pitched forward in a swirl of linen and creative ambition, landed flat in a tray of oily appetisers, and disappeared briefly behind a decorative net.

Someone in the crowd clapped.

At that precise moment, the fairy lights exploded in a synchronized chain reaction, one by one, like tiny theatrical betrayals.

The speaker let out a screech of feedback so aggressive it stunned the kittens, rattled the wine glasses, and sent Eleni muttering the Lord's Prayer backwards.

Then the wind arrived.

It wasn't much, just a well-timed, well-aimed gust from the hills, but it was enough.

Three dolphin-shaped cut-outs, suspended from fishing line, tore loose from their moorings and launched skyward.

The first flopped tragically into the herb patch.

The second struck the emergency bench, knocking Spiros's hat clean into his soup.

And the third, the largest, with googly eyes and laminated fins, looped twice through the air and embedded itself, point-first, in the wheel spokes of the priest's parked moped.

There was a silence.

A long one.

Claude groaned from somewhere under the netting, face glistening with olive tapenade and what might have been *tzatziki*.

Father Angelos, who had only just arrived and witnessed none of the preamble, stood frozen by his vehicle, hands raised as if being bombed by Poseidon.

Maria crossed herself and whispered, "This is how plagues start."

Spiros muttered, "We angered the dolphins."

And Alex, stepping carefully over the wreckage with a fork in one hand and a coffee in the other, said, "Well. That went better than expected."

Claude, rising slowly like a man reborn from calamity, announced, "I meant every moment."

Later, he would insist it was a performance piece.

Spiros, who had observed the entire thing from his usual seat under the vine (smoking, of course), finally stood up. He surveyed the disorder, the smouldering extension cord, Claude face-down in the sand, Maria giving CPR to a flan, and nodded sagely. "Best festival since the monarchy fell," he said, and sat back down.

The priest, meanwhile, would avoid the lemon grove for the next week and refuse to bless anything within twenty metres of dolphin foam board.

For the rest of the summer, tourists would pose with the moped.

Locals would leave offerings near the oregano patch.

And Maria would start bottling a new olive oil blend she called "Dolphin's Descent".

But on the night, nobody left. Why would they? There was fish (kind of), there was fire (briefly), and there was *tsipouro* (too much). Children danced barefoot. Old men argued about which dolphin was the most divine. Claude, somehow, got a standing ovation. Maria began planning next year's festival before dessert.

Alex, ever practical, declared, "We're never doing this again."

I quietly made a second napkin list titled "Things We Must Never Repeat". I ran out of ink by "squid flambé". But deep down, we knew the truth. It was ridiculous. It was chaotic. It was a health and safety violation in at least four categories. But it was also ours. And in the end, it didn't matter that the fish ran out, the stage collapsed, or that no dolphins were ever confirmed. What mattered was that the village was laughing again. And that? That's better than any blessing.

Even from a dolphin.

CHAPTER THIRTY-TWO

AMONG THE LEMONS

It's hard to describe the feeling of one of our perfect evenings in the lemon grove.

There was no music; Alex had forbidden it. "Let nature be the soundtrack," she'd said, waving off Claude's proposal for a live jazz-fusion trio with castanets.

So it was crickets and birds, the occasional buzz of a curious bee, and the soft clink of forks on ceramic. People spoke more quietly out there, not in reverence, but in response. Something about the grove made you lean in.

Lamps swayed. Leaves danced. And the lemons, hanging

stubbornly from their branches, glowed like forgotten moons.

It was peaceful. It was imperfect. It was exactly what we hadn't known we needed.

Zorba's had been open for a while now. Long enough for routines to settle, quirks to become systems, and disorganisation to be mistaken for charm.

We had the permits. The certificates. The stamps. Even the fire extinguisher had a name, a backstory, and a godparent.

What began as an experiment was, somehow, now a philosophy, lived, breathed, and occasionally shouted across the kitchen.

No one had written it down, of course. But we all knew the rules:

- Feed people well.
- Smile, even if it's hot.
- Never let Claude handle the wine list alone.
- And always, always pretend Spiros is in charge, even when he's asleep.

There were no foreign dishes. No imported truffle oil. No pizza. Zorba's served what we could find, grow, make, or fish. Theodora had made this law, and Theodora's laws were not to be broken unless you enjoyed being glared at in four dimensions.

So, the menu changed daily, depending on the sea, the season, and whether Dimitri had run out of petrol again. You didn't ask for a burger. You didn't request substitutions. You asked Theodora what she had cooked, and you thanked the gods if she smiled when telling you.

This wasn't a restaurant. It was a living, breathing extension of the village. A community table, stretched across sand and citrus.

At first it was just locals. Then friends of locals. Then tourists. Shy at first, apologetic, wondering if they were allowed.

They were. If they respected the rules:

1. Sit where you like.

2. Don't ask for ketchup.

3. If you don't know what something is, eat it and find out.

4. Always trust the woman in the apron.

5. And never, under any circumstances, move Theodora's pots.

They came for the food. They stayed for the story. They watched Spiros smoke under the fig tree and nod sagely at nothing in particular. They saw Claude debate metaphysics with

Katerina. They watched the kittens playing under the tables. They tasted Vassiliki's *bougatsa* and cried.

And most evenings, as the sun slipped behind the mountain and the grove turned golden, they realised that what we had built wasn't just a taverna. It was a small, sticky, crooked version of paradise.

Now, every night before the rush, Alex and I walk the path between the tables, brushing leaves off chairs, straightening candles, whispering thanks to no one in particular.

She usually stops beneath the biggest tree, the one Theodora insists grows the best liqueur lemons, and rests her hand against the bark. "It's ours now," she says sometimes.

And I always nod.

Because it is. Not by deed or signature. By care. By love. By dinner service and stubbornness. This grove. This village. This life.

Ours.

One evening, as I walked through the grove collecting empty plates, I paused beneath one of the older trees.

The sky was dusky pink. The last candle flickered low.

A family of Austrian tourists were sipping *tsipouro* in reverent silence. Claude had fallen asleep at his table, a scarf over his face and a cat curled on his lap.

Alex was laughing with Mary near the bar, her hair wild, her hands flour-dusted, her eyes bright. And I thought, this is it.

Peter Barber

It's not a taverna. Not a business. But a place. A little village within the village. With lemons. And love. And just enough madness to make it perfect.

CHAPTER THIRTY-THREE

Exit Strategies and Scratched Surfaces

If raising five kittens taught us anything, it was this: love is loud, sticky, and usually ends up in the biscuit tin.

They grew, of course. Kittens don't stay kittens any more than ouzo stays in the bottle after Maria's name day. And just when we'd all grown used to the daily stampede across tabletops, the shredded menus, and the odd mewling from inside the cutlery drawer… change arrived uninvited.

It started subtly. One cat stopped following Katerina to the compost heap. Another began spending afternoons lounging on Spiros's moped – not sleeping, but posing. As if auditioning for some cat calendar. Claude offered to photograph it for a postcard series. Spiros offered to run it over.

Then Up, our acrobatic table-jumper and proud destroyer of ceiling fans, disappeared for two days and returned with a fish. A whole fish. No one knew from where. Possibly the harbour. Possibly a rival taverna. He dropped it at Katerina's hooves like a sacrificial offering. She stared at it, unimpressed, then at him.

The message was clear: "*You're* feeding me *now*?"

Bit by bit, they began to drift.

Toe-Biter started spending nights on the church roof. Napkin developed a crush on a long-haired cat from the next village and began disappearing at suspicious intervals. Not Ours took to riding in baskets with the fruit delivery, jumping out at inopportune moments like a fuzzy landmine.

Souvlaki stayed loyal – if sticky – the longest. He still tried to drag chicken bones under chairs. He still slept on Katerina's back like a furry epaulette. But even he had moments, distant stares across the olive grove, long yawns in the lemon shade, that hinted at change.

And Katerina noticed.

She didn't say anything, obviously. She's a goat. But she watched. More than usual. Less of the dramatic headbutting, more quiet glances. She followed them from a distance. Not stalking – supervising. Like a very tired headmistress on playground duty.

Then came the day we knew was coming.

Napkin left.

Just… left. One afternoon he climbed onto the delivery van, curled up between the crates of vegetables, and rode off into the unknown. The driver didn't notice until halfway to the market. When he opened the back, there sat Napkin, smug, purring, and covered in coriander.

He stayed in the next village. Took up residence near the school canteen. Apparently, the headmistress there feeds him sardines and calls him "Professor Meow".

We broke the news gently.

Katerina was sprawled in her usual sunbeam near the kitchen door. We approached cautiously, like diplomats informing a queen that one of her ambassadors had defected.

"Napkin's moved on," I said. "New place. New name. Better fish."

She blinked.

Alex added, "We hear he's happy."

Katerina stood. Stretched. Snorted. Then she trotted off to the compost pile like we'd told her nothing more important than the weather.

But that night, she didn't sleep under the lemon tree. And the next morning, she headbutted an olive crate hard enough to crack it.

Even Claude, usually immune to subtlety, looked concerned. "She's grieving," he whispered. "She's been abandoned."

"She's a goat," said Mana, not unkindly. "It's just instinct.

Or wind."

But we all knew. This was more than wind.

The next to go was Not Ours. Naturally.

She left in style, jumping into the backseat of a German rental car and refusing to leave. The couple thought she was part of the local folklore and promised to send postcards. They named her "Athena" and bought her a travel cushion. She now lives in Berlin, and enjoys sauerkraut with her smoked salmon.

We barely had time to process that before Up got adopted by a yoga teacher from Thessaloniki. She claimed he had "meditative energy". This is the same cat who once bit through the Wi-Fi cable because it was humming too loudly.

By the time Toe-Biter and Souvlaki wandered off, one to a vineyard, the other to a boat, only Katerina remained.

She didn't mope. That's not her style. But she grew quieter. Slower. Spent longer chewing in silence. Took fewer naps under tables, and more up on the hill, where she could see the lemon trees, the taverna, and the paths they'd all taken away.

We gave her space.

Maria tried to get her to pose for new photos. She refused.

Eleni offered to register her as a "retired caregiver under domestic animal legislation". She didn't respond.

Mana brought her stale *koulourakia* and murmured things like "ungrateful little furballs" under her breath. But once, when she thought we weren't looking, she whispered, "They'll visit. You'll see."

And then… one did.

Months later. On a Sunday, just after the lunch rush.

Souvlaki.

He came trotting down the path like nothing had happened. He looked bigger. Sleeker. With a tiny bell someone had tied to his jewelled collar. He marched straight up to the kitchen door, meowed, and curled into Katerina's side like the prodigal goat-cat son he clearly was.

She didn't react for a long moment.

Then, with a great sigh and one slow nod, she licked his head. Then she licked him again. After that, we knew she'd be alright.

These days, some of the kittens-turned-cats visit now and then. They arrive like teenagers home for holidays. Hungry. Loud. Slightly cooler than they used to be. They stay a day or two, then disappear again, leaving behind pawprints, overturned bins, and half-eaten anchovies.

But whenever they do, Katerina is there. Waiting. Watching.

Because love doesn't leave. It expands. It makes room. Even if that room smells like fish and has claw marks in the napkin drawer.

So if you see a goat sitting quietly at the edge of the square, don't be fooled by the stillness. She's not alone.

She's just remembering the noise.

And waiting for the next unexpected box.

CHAPTER THIRTY-FOUR

THE MONEY BIT (UNFORTUNATELY)

Running a taverna, it turns out, is a lot like hosting a dinner party for eighty people. Every night. With no RSVP. And they all expect cheap drinks and possibly a goat.

At first, it seemed manageable. We had fish from Dimitri, cheese from George, pastries from Vassiliki, and the collective delusion that everything would somehow "work itself out".

But after a few weeks, cracks began to show. Not in the walls (Stamos had fixed those with leftover tiles and faith), but in our finances.

We were breaking even. Which sounds nice. Responsible.

Adult, even. Even when "even" included buying fish, paying for wine, electricity (when the grid felt generous), and replacing cutlery that had mysteriously vanished into the sea.

But there was one question that changed everything.

It happened on a Tuesday.

"So," Maria said, swirling her wine like a financial auditor, "are we... getting paid yet?"

I blinked. "Paid?"

"Yes," she said, in a tone usually reserved for interrogations or threatening to call someone's cousin at the town hall. "You know, money. Euros. Coin of the realm."

I opened my mouth to answer. George interrupted helpfully. "No one gets paid," he said cheerfully. "But we all suffer equally!" He was fine, he made the cheese and got paid for that, so he wasn't really expecting anything else.

He raised a glass. No one clinked.

Claude, having read three and a half articles on cooperative economics, decided we needed a formal meeting. He called it "a fiscal roundtable", and it took place under the olive tree with leftover tzatziki and a spreadsheet drawn in crayon.

"We are experiencing a liquidity issue," he announced, pointing solemnly to a bar graph made of breadsticks.

Alex sighed. "Claude. We have no money."

"Yes," he said proudly. "Which is what I said. But in French."

At this point, we faced a terrible truth. We were running a business. Which meant we had to *be* a business. Forming a cooperative in Greece is something like attempting to translate ancient Greek poetry while blindfolded, underwater, and waiting for a government clerk named Nikos who only works on Thursdays, except in August. Eleni, naturally, took the lead.

She returned from her first visit to the tax office white with rage and holding a stack of papers titled "Form A.1a, B.2c and Z (Draft Only)." We offered her wine and a chair. She accepted the wine and threatened to burn the chair.

Alex suggested we just declare the taverna a religion. Eleni didn't laugh. Father Evangelos frowned and looked at her over his spectacles.

At that point, Theodora and Mary were the only ones on the payroll. That was non-negotiable. They were the heart, hands, and voice of Zorba's. Without them, we'd be serving raw tomatoes, uncooked pasta, and *tsipouro* in espresso cups.

But now we had to decide who else, if anyone, should receive actual money rather than just praise, leftovers, and the occasional suspicious bottle of home-made liqueur.

Eleni?

Absolutely. Although she never asked, and she lived comfortably on her pension, we still felt she warranted something extra. She'd stared down the local bureaucracy and won, armed with nothing but a biro, a folder of forms, and the righteous fury of a woman who once corrected a priest's Greek.

Dimitri? Technically he was already being paid, in cash, kind, or occasionally diesel and buckets of lemons.

George? Officially, we paid him full price for his cheese, which was only fair, as it kept half the taverna coming back. Unofficially, he also received a steady supply of leftover bread for his goats, never saw a bill for wine, and occasionally got thanked in *tsipouro*. It wasn't a salary. But it worked.

Vassiliki? She refused cash but accepted strong coffee and constant praise.

Father Evangelos? He ate and drank for free and never once saw a bill. This was tradition, and also a strategic decision: he could bless us or bury us. Better to keep him full and cheerful.

Zorba? He didn't want rent, but we agreed that if we ever turned a real profit, we'd start giving him an envelope every month, containing cash, cheese, and possibly a bottle of Dimitri's lemon-infused *tsipouro* (Batch #4: Now with fewer hallucinations and you only *believed* you were blind, rather than it actually being true).

Alex and I? We didn't need paying. We had each other, a mountain of lemons, and the quiet satisfaction of watching other people argue instead of us.

Our proposed solutions:

- Raise prices? Mutiny.
- Add a cover charge? Spiros threatened revolution.
- Charge for water? Eleni said that was "illegal, immoral, and unforgivable".

- Claude suggested branded tote bags. Three were made. One was used to carry potatoes, one was stolen by a Swedish tourist, and the third became a hat for Katerina.

In the end, we abandoned formal wages for most in favour of something far older and far more Greek: barter, powered by appetite, whim, and mild confusion.

A single shift might earn you a full plate of food.

Mopping the floor bought you a drink, assuming the floor stayed wet for more than ten minutes.

Clearing a table without losing any cutlery usually resulted in an approving grunt from Theodora, the highest honour available.

Maria insisted on being paid in secrets.

Claude lobbied for a "stipend for ambiance", though no one could define what that meant and we suspected he couldn't either.

Dimitri asked if he could issue his own currency – Zorba Coins. When asked what they were worth, he shrugged and said, "Depends how thirsty you are."

No one understood the system, but somehow it worked.

Alex stood at the edge of the grove, notebook in hand, the glow of the setting sun framing her like a woman ready to declare a new political movement.

"We're not making a profit," she said.

"But we're still the talk of the village?" Maria asked.

"Yes," Alex nodded. "Because we serve food, *tsipouro*, and drama."

Claude murmured something about "artistic vision".

George wept softly into a cheese invoice.

Mary asked if she could have Wednesdays off (paid).

Spiros said nothing but was carving "I warned you" into his bench with a toothpick.

So, we would pay who we could and try to keep things running before the revolt.

That night, Zorba shuffled to his usual table, poured himself a *tsipouro* from behind the bar, and surveyed the scene.

"You're doing it wrong," he said, sipping slowly.

We all groaned.

"But," he added, with the ghost of a grin, "somehow… it's right."

And really, that was all we needed.

Chapter Thirty-Five

Holy Smoke, He's Got a Rocket Launcher

Easter in Greece is not a holiday. It's a seismic event. It's part ritual, part opera, and part pyrotechnic accident waiting to happen, garnished with *tsipouro* and served with love. It's a bit like joining a cult run by your grandmother, your most theatrical uncle, and a goat with attitude to make things truly perfect. There's incense, explosions, theological prayers, flower petals, and enough food to feed a small navy.

Good Friday began with optimism and poor measurement skills.

Zorba's Parthenon - A Taverna by the Sea

The *Epitaphios*, Christ's flower-laden funeral bier, had been constructed and decorated inside the church with such love and care that no one thought to check whether it would actually fit through the door. It did not.

There followed thirty minutes of muttered geometry, several conflicting opinions shouted at once, and at least three sprigs of jasmine being sacrificed to the cause. Theodora crossed herself. Stamos offered to "redesign the doorway".

Eventually, after dismantling half the handles and tilting the entire structure sideways while Alex supervised like an air traffic controller at an Orthodox airport, the *Epitaphios* was freed.

A round of spontaneous applause broke out. Zorba muttered, "Like every year." Which was probably true. And so we began. A solemn midnight procession, candles in hand, weaving through the village streets.

Brown beeswax candles flickered against the wind. Children darted between legs. Old ladies recited psalms like secret recipes. Cats led the way as if they had been appointed to guide souls.

Then came the fireworks. At first, I frowned. I mean, this was a funeral procession – granted, a temporary one, but still. Then I saw who was launching the pyrotechnics: it was Father Evangelos, robes flowing, candle in one hand, a firework in the other, grinning like a schoolboy lighting his first banger.

One especially loud crack echoed around the mountainside. The priest looked innocent. Too innocent. That kind of innocent that says, "Yes, I lit it, but can you prove it?" He gave us all the "Who, me?" look while discreetly blowing on his fingers like a gunslinger.

The next evening we all assembled at midnight back at the church. The church lights dimmed.

A hush fell. Then came the flame. Brought from the tomb of Christ in Jerusalem, flown by plane, candle, priest, and car to our tiny corner of Greece. It passed out of the church to the assembled crowd from hand to hand, candle to candle. From the priest to Claude, to Eleni, to Maria, to us.

The flame grew, flickered, danced, the light of resurrection, passed with murmurs of "*Christos Anesti!*" (Christ is risen.) We answered: "*Alithós Anésti.*" (Truly, He is risen.)

Even Spiros whispered it, his eyes glinting behind the candlelight.

And then, as the church bells struck midnight, the sky exploded.

Not your average municipal fireworks. Not even the rogue backyard display from the night before, courtesy of Father Evangelos and a suspicious cardboard box. This time, it was an organised show.

Sort of.

The first explosion rattled the wine glasses.

The second sent three cats under the tables and one tourist under Maria's apron.

Rockets burst over the rooftops, scattering sparks across

the olive trees. The lemon grove was briefly illuminated in holy strobe.

Claude dived behind the bougainvillea, shrieking "*Liberté!*" like a man reliving a different kind of revolution.

It was glorious, echoing, wide-eyed excitement. Every bang seemed to wake the hills. Every flare painted the whitewashed walls with light and noise and resurrection. Children cheered. Grandmothers crossed themselves. Someone lit a candle with a sparkler and declared it a miracle.

And just like that, Easter had arrived.

Katerina ran through the square wearing a paper crown she had stolen from a child. No one stopped her. She looked fabulous.

The tourists, wide-eyed and unsure whether they'd accidentally wandered onto a movie set, clapped nervously.

Then, just as suddenly, it stopped.

The flames flickered. The smoke cleared. And the scent of lamb began to drift from kitchens across the village. Most of us had fasted for forty days. That's forty days without meat, dairy, or joy. So what's the first thing we eat?

Magiritsa.

A thick, lemony soup made from the lamb's liver, lungs, heart, kidneys, and whatever else could be respectfully scraped out and sanctified with dill and rice. It sounds alarming. It tastes divine. At least, it does at 1 a.m. after several glasses of wine and a spiritual awakening via fireworks. George called it "medicine for the soul". Claude called it "delicately violent". Dimitri added more lemon and said, "Now it's perfect."

Alex handed out bowls like a general distributing rations, eyes still shining from the procession.

I ate two bowls. I have no shame.

The next morning, or more accurately, six hours later, the village came alive again. In every garden, lambs turned on spits, basted with lemon and oregano. Smoke coiled over fences. Music began to play. Dimitri brought out home-made wine he swore was aged (it wasn't). Claude wore a festive cravat. Maria brought salad and gossip. And in the centre of it all: *kokoretsi*.

For the uninitiated, *kokoretsi* is a cylindrical wonder made by wrapping lamb intestines around seasoned offal like a particularly bold meat scroll.

By midday, everyone was full.

By 2 p.m., most had wandered home for naps and digestion.

Except for Katerina, who was still wearing her crown and eyeing the leftovers like a goat-shaped monarch, and a handful of stragglers too full to move or too happy to leave.

Alex and I sat on the patio of the taverna. Smoke in the air. Music rising. Laughter drifting back from the lemon grove. It wasn't a crowd anymore – just the kind of people who stay behind to help clear plates and open one last bottle.

Friends. Family. Ours.

Alex leaned her head on my shoulder. "Chaos," she whispered.

"Perfection," I said.

Because Easter in a Greek village isn't just a holiday. It's proof that life, like lamb, is best when slow-roasted with love and just the right amount of oregano.

CHAPTER THIRTY-SIX

GHOSTS OF THE GROVE

One moonlit evening, Maria was to be found standing outside the taverna, hands on hips, eyes narrowed at the lemon grove as if it had insulted her cousin.

"I'm telling you," she whispered dramatically, "I heard something."

"What kind of something?" asked George, who was mostly just trying to finish his wine.

"A *presence*," Maria replied. "Something unnatural."

"It was probably Katerina," I said. "She snores."

Maria shook her head. "No. This was male. Deep. Tragic.

Like a forgotten poem."

Claude, who had been eavesdropping with the intensity of a man hoping to discover a ghost who quoted Baudelaire, gasped audibly.

From that moment, the lemon grove was no longer a shady seating area.

It was a portal. A mystery. Possibly haunted. Definitely gossip-worthy.

By morning, the story had ripened like fruit in the sun.

Maria told Eleni.

Eleni told Theodora.

Theodora told Father Evangelos, who nodded gravely and began polishing his incense holder.

"It could be old Uncle Stavros," said Spiros, unprompted. "He used to nap under those trees."

"Wasn't he the one who vanished?" asked Mary.

"No," said Spiros. "That was Uncle Lefteris. Stavros just married badly and took up beekeeping."

"Same difference," said Maria.

By lunch, the ghost had a name, a personality, and a tragic backstory involving unrequited love, lemon schnapps, and a failed attempt to woo a French opera singer who was visiting the island "for her nerves". None of it was true. But it didn't matter.

Within days, Claude announced he would be conducting a séance. "For cultural enrichment," he said, "and emotional closure."

"For chaos," muttered Alex.

He arrived wearing a flowing white shirt and a scarf with moons on it, and carrying a baguette for reasons no one questioned. He lit candles (too many), burned sage (accidentally), and seated six volunteers around a makeshift table beneath the oldest lemon tree.

Katerina joined. Uninvited. Naturally.

Claude dimmed the lanterns. The crickets hushed. A breeze whispered through the grove.

"Is anyone here?" he called to the darkness.

A lemon dropped with perfect comic timing.

Maria gasped. George dropped his glass. Eleni crossed herself three times and declared that her left foot had gone cold.

Claude closed his eyes and whispered, "Stavros, if that's you… knock once."

The wind knocked over the wine bottle.

That was all anyone needed.

By the next morning, Dimitri was bottling what he claimed was "lemon spirit essence" in recycled water bottles with handmade labels that read, "Grove No. 7 – Hauntingly Smooth."

"It's for protection," he said, pouring a suspiciously clear liquid into small vials. "Or refreshment. Depending on the mood."

"Is it safe?" I asked.

Dimitri shrugged. "Mostly."

Claude insisted it be used before each séance. Maria took one home to "cleanse her cousin's aura". Father Evangelos refused to comment.

One tourist drank it by accident and said he could hear other people's dreams. We asked whose. He just stared at the lemon tree.

We never quite knew what was in it. We didn't ask again.

Soon, the hysteria reached its peak.

Someone claimed to see a glowing figure walking between the trees at dusk. (We later discovered it was Vassiliki, wearing a reflective raincoat and sneaking figs.)

Someone else heard crying near the water tank. (It turned out to be George after having read the electricity bill.)

But the whispers continued.

The grove, once peaceful, became charged. Full of glances, stories, and teenagers daring each other to sleep there overnight. Claude began sketching plans for a "spirit garden". Maria suggested charging tourists extra to sit near "the haunted lemon". Eleni insisted we register the grove as a historical site.

It was Zorba who finally ended it.

He wandered into the grove one evening, leaned on his cane, and sat beneath the fourth tree, the one Maria claimed was definitely cursed.

He lit a cigarette. Sipped his *tsipouro*. Waited.

After a long silence, he called out into the dark, "If you're here, ghost... I planted these damn lemons. So make yourself useful and prune something."

Nothing happened.

He nodded once, stood up, and walked away.

The ghost, it seemed, had been exorcised. Or possibly it got bored.

Peace (sort of) returned. The séance table became a regular dining table again. The candles were used for birthday cakes.

Claude moved on to astrology.

Maria moved on to her cousin's divorce.

Dimitri's lemon spirit sold out.

And the grove?

It went back to being what it always was.

A slightly overgrown, oddly magical place full of fruit, gossip, laughter, and mystery.

Maybe it was haunted.

Maybe not.

But it didn't matter.

Because in a village like ours, even the ghosts are welcome, as long as they don't mess with Theodora's kitchen or sit in Zorba's chair.

CHAPTER THIRTY-SEVEN

A Name Day to Remember

If you've never experienced a Greek name day celebration, imagine a birthday party, a religious holiday, a village-wide food festival, and mild political unrest, all rolled into one, and hosted by someone who insists "it's no big deal" while roasting a whole lamb and setting a table for fifty relatives.

In Greece, your name day – the feast day of the saint you're named after – is often more important than your actual birthday. And since every person in the village is named after a saint, these events happen *often*, and *loudly*.

So when Father Evangelos stood up during Sunday liturgy and announced that *this year*, the village would be hosting a proper celebration for Saint Evangelos, we knew we were in trouble.

Not because we didn't want to honour him. But because, in typical Greek fashion, he added, "I've invited some friends from the mainland."

"How many?" someone asked.

"Just a few," he said.

This would translate, of course, to, two boatloads, and one distant cousin who brought a sound system and a box of fireworks labelled "legal (possibly)".

The taverna became the de facto headquarters. Zorba claimed he'd seen a name day like this once before and it ended with a pig in the priest's bathtub.

Maria began drawing up guest lists on napkins. Eleni started drafting a legal waiver. George offered his cheese "at cost", which is Greek for "as long as I get to pick the music".

Alex, naturally, took charge.

"We'll need seating for at least 150," she said.

"In the lemon grove?" I asked.

"In the lemon grove, the road, the beach, and possibly Dimitri's fishing boat," she replied.

Dimitri blinked. "Do I need to move the nets?"

"Yes," said Alex. "Also, what's that smell?"

"Fish," Dimitri replied. It wasn't.

The problem with village-wide celebrations is that they bring together people who haven't spoken since 1994. Like Eleni and Spiros, who still weren't on speaking terms after the infamous cemetery dispute.

There was also the matter of Theodora and Vassiliki's long-standing quarrel over which family invented almond biscuits. Both began baking furiously, and by midday it looked like a flour bomb had gone off in the taverna.

Mary took the opportunity to flirt shamelessly with the new baker's apprentice from the next village, who wore cologne so strong it gave Claude a nosebleed.

"I think I'm in love," she sighed.

"With him or the cologne?" I asked.

"Yes," she said.

The feast preparations reached biblical proportions. Three lambs were spit-roasted on borrowed machinery. Eleni brought 187 *dolmades* and a warning label. Claude attempted a "fusion baklava" with French cheese. It was politely buried behind the compost heap. Dimitri brewed a barrel of something so strong the varnish bubbled off the serving table.

Father Evangelos, meanwhile, remained calm.

He blessed the bread. He blessed the lamb. He blessed a woman's sprained ankle. At one point, he even blessed the tablecloth after someone spilled *tsipouro* on it.

"It's important to cover all bases," he said, sipping from a mysterious jar someone had handed him.

By sunset, the taverna was transformed.

We'd expected around 150 people. Give or take a few.

What we got was exactly 150, plus everyone's cousin, neighbour, ex-boyfriend, and that one woman who once bought a jar of olives and now thinks she's a shareholder.

They came in sandals and linen, dragging extra chairs from parked cars, dropping off bottles with suspicious labels, and kissing Maria like returning saints. They didn't book. They simply arrived, smiling, hungry, and entirely confident someone else would sort it out.

The taverna filled in minutes.

The lemon grove followed.

The small patch of land between the bins and the oregano planter was decreed "Table Twelve" and someone wrote it down.

Claude tried to seat a couple on the water barrel and called it *rustic elevation*.

A tourist asked if we had a vegan meze board and was met with polite silence and one boiled egg.

Theodora, to her credit, knew she couldn't face it alone.

She'd seen the guest list. She'd felt the temperature rising, not just in the kitchen, but in her knees. And she'd muttered something about "not being twenty" before marching off to recruit like a general with a ladle.

She brought in reinforcements: two cooks from a taverna in the next village, which happened to be closed that day – whether by coincidence or because Theodora *closed it*, we didn't ask;

a cousin from Crete who had flown in for a quiet holiday and now found herself elbow-deep in batter, rethinking her family ties; and two of someone's daughters, no one could remember whose, who tied on aprons and declared they could cook "like *yiayia* taught us", which could mean anything from Michelin-starred brilliance to dangerous improvisation.

Inside, the kitchen teetered on the sacred edge between divine inspiration and full-blown emergency. Theodora and Mary moved like orchestrated chaos, arms flying, pots slamming, spoons clattering, flour rising in glorious, airborne defiance of gravity. The guest chefs were already shouting. The Cretan cousin was arguing with the oven. Someone lit a burner with a prayer. Someone else screamed for more aubergines. One pot boiled over. Another wouldn't boil at all. A lump of feta flew through the air, hit a cupboard, and was caught mid-sentence by one of the mystery daughters, who gave a thumbs up and kept stirring.

At one point, Alex poked her head in.

She stood there for three seconds, took in the smoke, the shouting, the strange humming noise coming from somewhere behind the fridge, then nodded slowly and said, "Excellent. No one's crying yet." Then she turned and walked out before anyone could hand her a chopping board.

And through it all, Theodora stayed calm. Not peaceful, but *controlled*. The kind of calm that comes from absolute authority and knowing exactly where the good knives are hidden.

Because if anyone dropped the tray of *spanakopita*, there would be consequences. And we all knew it.

We were running out of plates.

Desperation set in. So we offered a glass of Dimitri's *tsipouro* to anyone willing to take a turn at the washing-up station.

The locals, wise and weary, politely declined. They knew Dimitri's *tsipouro*. They respected it. They avoided it like they'd avoid an open manhole on a rainy night.

But the tourists?

Bright-eyed. Eager. Unaware. They stepped forward like heroes, thrilled by the idea of an *authentic experience.*

Mugs.

In every sense of the word.

The wine bottles with labels had run out. Dimitri had started pouring from unlabelled ones.

Katerina had appointed herself manager of morale and leftovers. She patrolled the grove like a slightly tipsy security guard, accepting handouts, headbutting the wine crate, and gently menacing a woman from Thessaloniki who tried to pet her mid-chew. At one point, she climbed onto the low wall by Table Eight, stared directly into the eyes of a German tourist, and stole a stuffed vine leaf without blinking.

We did what Greek villages have always done in times of festive collapse: we recruited. People expecting a quiet dinner were pressed into service without ceremony. If you were holding a napkin, you were now a waiter. If you could open a bottle, you were promoted to sommelier.

One grandmother was mid-sip of wine when she was handed a chopping board and a mission. She didn't protest, she just adjusted her headscarf and asked, "Where's the garlic?"

Teenagers were conscripted into the grove with trays. Younger children were assigned "floor-level observation and napkin patrol". One of them earned a standing ovation for single-handedly retrieving a runaway tomato before it made it into the herb garden.

Eleni ran the till, the music, and a simultaneous argument about feta portions. George tested the wine. Thoroughly. Claude vanished for twenty minutes and returned smelling of fried cheese.

And still, somehow, the food arrived.

Not always at the right table. Not always warm. But it arrived.

Laughter climbed over the plates. Chairs shifted and multiplied. And the night rose with the heat and the music and that strange village feeling that nothing works, yet everything happens.

By the end, no one could tell who had come to eat and who had been drafted into service. No one cared.

Even Theodora allowed herself a sit-down, for four and a half minutes.

Mary was seen leaning on a doorframe, eating a cold *dolma* with one hand and gesturing with the other.

Lanterns flickered between the lemon trees. Plates clinked. Glasses overflowed. Children ran wild. Music poured into the night like it had nowhere else to go.

People danced. People argued. Some cried, apologised, then danced again.

Claude gave a short, mostly ignored speech about the sanctity of tradition. Dimitri translated it as, "Let's all drink."

Zorba stood quietly near the grill, nodding in rhythm with the *bouzouki*, a *tsipouro* in one hand, the other keeping Katerina from chewing the priest's robes.

At some point late into the night, someone noticed Spiros had gone missing.

A brief panic ensued. Search parties were formed. Flashlights flickered across the olive grove. Claude suggested a séance.

Eventually, we found him asleep inside the old bread oven, curled up like a saintly kebab, snoring peacefully with a slice of cheese still in his pocket.

"He's fine," said Father Evangelos. "Just spiritually overwhelmed."

Like all great Greek celebrations, it ended not with a bang, but with the scraping of chairs, the clink of empty glasses, and the soft sigh of a village well-fed, well-loved, and slightly fermented.

The moon rose. The crickets resumed their song. Alex collapsed onto a bench, triumphant and exhausted.

"That," she said, "was tough."

"That," I replied, "was magical."

And somewhere in the lemon grove, a goat burped, and all was well.

CHAPTER THIRTY-EIGHT

STRANGERS AT THE GATE

Something small and buzzing had arrived. But this one didn't have legs or try to suck blood. It was worse: it was a drone, a buzzing, overly confident drone that hovered above the lemon grove one breezy afternoon, whirring like a mosquito with a real estate license.

Alex spotted it first.

"Is that... a toy?" she asked, shading her eyes.

Dimitri, who was mid-fishing-net-untangle and halfway through a detailed complaint about the lack of proper *tsipouro* etiquette, stopped cold.

"That," he growled, "is trouble."

Within minutes, the whole village had gathered. George pointed at it like it was a bad omen. Theodora crossed herself twice. Maria called her cousin in the next village to see if they'd had any mysterious aerial visitors. They had. One crashed into a chicken coop.

Claude, of course, was thrilled. "It's art!" he declared.

"No," said Eleni, arriving with a folder. "It's a drone from a property firm in Athens. I recognise the logo."

"How?" I asked.

"They tried to buy my brother's farm. Claimed they were building an 'eco-retreat experience.'" She spat the last word like it was something you caught from dirty water.

The drone disappeared over the hills. But it had left something behind. A sense. A tingle. A disturbance in the lemons.

Then came the men in chinos. A pair of smooth-faced, smooth-talking, suspiciously moisturised individuals appeared at the taverna. They wore sunglasses, carried iPads, and had the gall to order bottled water. Bottled. Water. That had come from a spring that was less than a kilometre away.

Alex greeted them politely. Maria greeted them with silence. Katerina attempted to eat one of their laces.

"We're exploring sustainable tourism opportunities in underutilised coastal areas," one said, in perfect English with the kind of accent that suggested too much time in boardrooms and not enough time in the sun.

Claude perked up. "Ah, but the soul of the village must be preserved."

The taller one smiled. "Of course. That's the whole idea. Authenticity sells."

That phrase landed like a dead fish on the bar.

Theodora narrowed her eyes. "Authenticity… sells?"

"Yes. The idea is to keep everything charming and traditional. But you know… clean. Refined. Curated."

Dimitri choked on his olive.

"You mean sterilised," Eleni snapped.

They didn't flinch.

"We're particularly interested in land adjacent to community spaces," one of them said, flipping through his tablet like it contained secrets. "Unused plots, that sort of thing. Like… that grove behind here?"

Every head turned to the lemon grove.

Zorba, who had been sitting quietly until then, made a sound somewhere between a grunt and a historical objection. It echoed.

Alex leaned forward. "It's not unused."

"It's quite used," I added. "It's lemon-scented and very popular with bees, and we use it for tables."

The man tapped his screen. "Yes, we saw that. The taverna and the grove are both listed under a Mr Zorba Papadakis?"

Alex nodded. "Correct."

"Is he available to speak with us?"

There was a silence. *The kind of silence that says: We're thinking about lying, but we haven't agreed on the details yet.*

Zorba folded his arms, said nothing, and looked the other way.

Note: Zorba never liked to admit ownership of anything – especially land. It attracted paperwork, taxes, and people with clipboards. Also, he was deeply suspicious of anyone wearing good shoes. They were usually tax inspectors. Or lawyers. Or worse, relatives.

The effect was not unlike a mountain deciding not to move or announce himself.

The men left soon after, with polite smiles. But something had shifted.

The next morning, flyers appeared, left on tables, tucked under windscreen wipers, one bold enough to be wedged into the crack of Zorba's closed shutter.

They showed images. Not of the village as it was, but of a village reimagined. Renderings of tidy bungalows with infinity pools. A beach bar called "Mythos Lounge". Someone had replaced the lemon grove with a wellness spa. There was a couple in yoga poses under a digitally rendered fig tree that was suspiciously symmetrical.

"No fig tree looks like that," said George. "They're messy. Like life."

We gathered at the taverna that night. Every villager. Even Father Evangelos, who blessed the ouzo before pouring two shots and calling the flyers "the work of demons with graphic design skills".

Alex said little, just stared at the paper until her knuckles whitened.

Then she stood. "We will not be curated," she said.

Claude raised a glass. "To disorder!"

"To goats!" Maria added.

"To the real," said Theodora. "Warts, weeds and all."

And so we sat, beneath the fairy lights, beneath the stars, and the lemon trees that were ours, but not on paper. Not in law. Not to the drone. And not to the men with pamphlets promising organic poolside serenity.

But we knew. And they knew. And we knew that they knew. They were circling. Which meant we needed a plan. And someone needed to speak to Zorba.

Because the grove and taverna might have been unclaimed on the land registry, but it wasn't unclaimed in our hearts. And if anyone was going to decide its future, it wouldn't be someone in chinos, and a drone.

It would be us.

CHAPTER THIRTY-NINE

THE GREAT *TSIPOURO* WAR

Every village in Greece has two things: a church, and at least six people who claim to make the *best tsipouro* on the island.

Our village had fourteen.

For years, the matter of whose tsipouro was best was a simmering background debate. A low-level, ever-present hum of bragging, whispering, and suspicious bottle-swapping.

Until, one warm Thursday afternoon, Dimitri ruined everything.

He swaggered into the taverna, dusty from the road, a battered glass bottle in one hand, and a grin that practically announced *impending disaster*.

"This," he declared, slamming the bottle onto the bar, "is the finest *tsipouro* in the region. Possibly the world."

"You say that every week," said George, not looking up.

"This time, it's true," Dimitri insisted. "New recipe. Triple distilled. Lemon-infused. Tastes like sunshine and petrol. Perfect."

Claude sniffed the bottle and promptly lost his sense of smell.

Theodora, overhearing from the kitchen, emerged wielding a ladle like a sceptre. "Yours tastes like paraffin," she snapped. "My cousin Elpida's *tsipouro* won gold in Thessaloniki."

"In 1978," George muttered.

"And she still uses the same barrel," Theodora said proudly.

A hush fell over the room.

It had begun.

Naturally, the village divided into factions. Everyone backed their favourite brewer:

Team Dimitri – for those who believed in bold experimentation, questionable hygiene, and bottles with no labels but very strong opinions. His supporters claimed his *tsipouro* could power a tractor or summon a vision of your grandfather.

Team Elpida – for supporters of Theodora's cousin from the hills, a tiny woman with monumental eyebrows and a still so well hidden no one had actually seen it. Her *tsipouro* tasted like truth, and possibly revenge.

Team Claude – for the romantics, the dreamers, the misguided tourists. Claude had attempted to infuse his batch with lavender, thyme, and a haiku. It was described by Dimitri as "hand lotion with feelings". He was politely booed.

Team Maria – for the teetotallers, accountants, and those who understood power. Maria didn't drink a drop, yet somehow acquired controlling shares in three barrels, issued tasting tokens, and instituted a loyalty card scheme.

Team Spiros – consisting solely of Spiros, who hadn't produced a drop but managed to sample every bottle. He claimed to support "unity through alcohol" and described himself as "Switzerland, but thirstier".

In time, an unofficial *Tsipouro* Tribunal was formed, chaired by Eleni, naturally, who brought a ledger, a tasting spoon, and the authority of someone who once audited the church accounts and lived to tell the tale.

Decisions were made.

Notes were taken.

No one agreed.

And more bottles appeared.

Even Father Evangelos was drawn in. He tried to remain neutral, but someone spotted him sipping from a suspicious flask during mass.

"Just for communion," he explained, eyes slightly unfocused.

Alex, sensing an incoming riot, called a village meeting.

"We'll have a proper competition," she announced. "A tasting. Blind. Fair. Civilised."

"This is *tsipouro*," Dimitri whispered. "Nothing about it is civilised."

Claude volunteered to coordinate. He brought scorecards, wine glasses, and a tiny bell.

"Why the bell?" someone asked.

"For ambiance," Claude said. "And judgment."

On the evening of the Great *Tsipouro* War, Zorba's taverna transformed from seaside charm to chemical warfare tasting lab.

Eight bottles stood like glass grenades on the judging table. Unlabelled. Uneven. One was still warm. All of them shimmered slightly, as though daring the laws of physics to interfere.

The villagers lined up like soldiers at dawn, wary, jittery, most clutching their glasses as if heading into combat.

The first round was cautious. Sip. Swirl. Stare into the middle distance. Repeat. Gag quietly.

By the third round, things had escalated.

Lips went numb. Tongues changed texture. One man turned slightly green and began quoting Sophocles. Another sneezed fire. Actual fire. A local dentist declared, "I no longer believe in enamel."

Maria was writing notes furiously, in what appeared to be Morse code.

George claimed he could "taste the earth", then accused someone of bottling the *tsipouro* directly from a tractor radiator.

Theodora slapped Elpida with a tea towel over an alleged copper coil conspiracy. Elpida retaliated by flinging oregano and shouting, "That's why your *tsipouro* tastes like furniture polish!"

Claude, having tasted four samples, reported he could see in chords, and began conducting the moon with a rosemary sprig.

Dimitri's infamous Lemon Grove Special made one unfortunate German tourist hiccup so violently he began singing "O Tannenbaum" through his nose. Spiros, having sampled everything twice, declared them all "excellent" before passing out on the olive scale. It was the calmest he'd looked all year.

By midnight, several contestants had forgotten what they'd submitted. One bottle was vibrating. The goat was licking another.

Still, Maria tallied votes with the solemnity of a war tribunal. Alex paced. Theodora crossed herself twice.

Finally, the numbers were in.

A tie.

Not between Dimitri and Elpida – who by now were both claiming victory in alternating dialects – but between Bottle #7, submitted anonymously, and Bottle #3, which no one remembered submitting.

Maria denied everything.

Claude had gone into a trance and was reading people's fortunes using a spoon.

George demanded a recount, then sobbed into his feta.

Theodora threatened to boil the results in a vat of lentils.

Alex, seeking peace (and plausible deniability), retrieved both mystery bottles and popped the corks.

She sniffed. Paused. Sighed.

"They're from Zorba's cupboard," she said. "He forgot he had them. They've been there since 1987."

A stunned silence followed. Even Katerina froze mid-chew.

Zorba, who hadn't entered, hadn't brewed since he gave us the taverna, hadn't even blinked all evening, lifted his glass slowly.

"You amateurs," he muttered, "overcomplicate everything."

And with that, he won the war he never fought.

There were no trophies, only hangovers. And a new village rule: no more than one *tsipouro* competition per year. Maybe. Probably.

But for now, the taverna was alive with stories, arguments, blurry memories, and a faint scent of citrus and rocket exhaust.

The war had ended. But the myth? That would last forever.

Because in the end, *tsipouro* isn't just a drink. It's a declaration. A tradition. A slightly dangerous act of faith.

And in this village, it's best served with a spoonful of rivalry, a splash of history, and a fire extinguisher nearby.

The next morning, the taverna resembled a battlefield where no one had died but several had deeply regretted living.

Chairs were on their sides. A broom was floating in the sea. Claude was asleep under Table Three, wrapped in a flag no one recognised, mumbling something about "the existential flavour of despair".

Maria appeared wearing sunglasses and wielding a notepad as if prepared to sue someone on moral grounds. "Someone," she said, pointing vaguely, "should apologise for last night's hallucinations. I spoke fluent Albanian and flirted with a moped."

George had developed a twitch in his left eyebrow and refused to discuss "the bottle with the heat". He sat in silence, nursing a yoghurt and whispering to it like a therapist.

Dimitri, undeterred, announced a new line of wellness *tsipouro*, allegedly infused with volcanic rock, saffron, and something he only referred to as "local inspiration". He branded it "Volcano Tears". Katerina headbutted the bottle off the table. Applause followed.

Elpida turned up with a notebook and declared she'd submitted an application for "Protected Geographical Indication" for her *tsipouro*, which she now referred to as "Heritage Firewater".

Maria accused her of cultural fraud.

Theodora demanded a tasting rematch under EU supervision.

Claude suggested holding a *Tsipouro* and Poetry Night. No one responded.

Zorba, as always, arrived at 11 a.m. He sat down, poured his own drink, glanced at the arguing crowd, the twisted chairs, the goat licking a postcard, and smiled.

He raised his glass. "To forgetting." Then he added, after a pause: "And then remembering it fondly."

No one knew exactly what he meant, but everyone agreed.

By sunset, the signs for next month's event were already being painted in four languages, by three rival teams – and one suspiciously artistic goat.

Because this is Greece.

And *tsipouro*, like revenge, love, and excellent *saganaki*, is best served slightly warm, entirely unregulated, and shared with people you'll almost certainly be arguing with again next week.

CHAPTER FORTY

Father Evangelos vs. the Octopus

Blessings, in a Greek village, are not to be taken lightly. Particularly if they come from Father Evangelos, who, despite being one of the gentlest souls on the island, has the authority of a small archangel and the patience of a saint with mild hay fever.

He had decided, quite solemnly, that Zorba's spiritually chaotic taverna required a formal ecclesiastical blessing. Not just of the building, or the tables, or the shaky extension cord running from the lemon grove to the bar. No, everything needed blessing. Specifically. Personally.

"I've blessed marriages, boats, goats and once a yoga retreat," he said. "It's time the taverna received its own."

And so, on a Tuesday morning when the sea was calm, the breeze smelled of wild mint, and Eleni had only shouted once before breakfast, Father Evangelos arrived in full ceremonial mode.

He was met at the door by Dimitri, who had just come back from a fishing trip, his arms full of gear, his hair full of seaweed, and his grin far too proud. "I brought something special," Dimitri announced.

He held up a bucket. The bucket sloshed. Something moved inside it.

Alex, who had just finished polishing cutlery with all the righteous fury of a woman managing a cooperative kitchen run by artists, eccentrics and semi-legal fishermen, narrowed her eyes.

"What's in the bucket?"

"Octopus," Dimitri beamed. "Fresh. Alive. Very clever." The bucket shifted again.

"Did you name it?" asked Mary, already inching behind a chair.

"Not yet. Thought we'd let it earn one," Dimitri said.

And then, of course, the bucket tipped. And the octopus, apparently having pondered escape during the entire journey from the net to the taverna, launched itself across the kitchen tiles with a squelching heroism rarely seen outside of Olympic sports.

Maria screamed. Claude dropped his coffee. George stood on a stool. Theodora grabbed a ladle and shouted, "This is why we need lids on things!"

And in the middle of it all, calm as a monastery bell, stood Father Evangelos.

He looked at the octopus. He looked at Dimitri. He looked at the chaos. And then, slowly, he reached into his satchel and pulled out the holy water.

"Are you going to bless it?" I asked, keeping a respectful distance in case the creature was also capable of flight.

"I'm considering it," the priest said. "Though I'm not entirely sure it wants to be saved."

The octopus paused on the floor, its limbs twitching as if calculating whether conversion was worth it.

"What does the Church say about molluscs?" asked Claude, always eager to intellectualise animal encounters.

"God created all creatures," said Father Evangelos. "But I believe the octopus was made on a Friday, when the Lord was tired and felt experimental."

There was a long silence. Then Dimitri tried to capture it with a colander. It inked him in the face.

"Unholy!" he howled, stumbling backwards and knocking over a stack of chairs.

Father Evangelos raised an eyebrow. "Perhaps a minor exorcism first," he mused.

Eventually – three brooms, a net, two broken tiles and one sacrificial mop later – the octopus was returned to its bucket, looking deeply unimpressed.

The priest stepped forward, sprinkled holy water over the kitchen, paused at the fridge, gave it an extra splash for safety, and then turned solemnly to Dimitri. "In future, keep your creatures outside during blessings," he said.

"Is it cursed?" Dimitri asked, still blinking black ink from his lashes.

"No," said Father Evangelos. "Just… unconvinced."

Later, over meze and wine, the incident sparked an impromptu theological discussion under the lemon trees.

Claude insisted the octopus was simply misunderstood – a gentle philosopher in suckered form, dragged unfairly into our world.

Maria claimed it was the ghost of an ancient monk, returning to test our moral fibre (and possibly our plumbing).

Theodora took one look at it, shrugged, and said if it stayed fresh, she'd stew it in wine and onions and give thanks to Saint Kalamaris.

Father Evangelos, who had seen much and commented rarely, smiled serenely. He poured himself a modest glass of *tsipouro*, held it up like a sacrament, and said, "In life, we must learn to make peace with many things. Bureaucracy. Broken roof tiles. Unexpected cousins arriving at midnight. And sometimes… a morally ambiguous cephalopod."

So we did the only sensible thing. We walked it back to the shore like a guest who'd overstayed, whispered a few words of uncertain Greek, and released it gently into the sea.

We couldn't eat something that had now been christened, spiritually debated, and possibly granted honorary sainthood.

Besides, there's only so much divine intervention one can digest before dinner.

But its memory lingered, in stains on the tiles, stories over *retsina*, and a cautious look that Father Evangelos now gives every bucket that crosses the taverna threshold.

Because at Zorba's, even blessings come with tentacles. And occasionally, theology bites back.

CHAPTER FORTY-ONE

CLAUDE'S CULTURAL COUP

E very village needs a Claude. Someone who quotes philosophers in the bakery queue.
Someone who wears scarves in July. Someone who believes, sincerely, that what a seaside taverna truly lacks is just a little *je ne sais quoi*.

Claude, our resident Franco-Hellenic romantic, had been mostly tolerated by the village on account of his harmless eccentricities, his noble moustache, and his tendency to pay for his wine in exact change. But one summer afternoon, with the sun too hot and the *tsipouro* a little too strong, Claude made an announcement that would echo across the lemon grove and ignite a minor culinary war.

"I shall host," Claude declared, standing beside the olive barrel as though it were a podium, "a night of French–Greek cultural fusion!"

The taverna fell silent.

Claude had that look in his eye again. The same look he'd had before the jazz night, the spoken-word olive tasting, and the incident with the live pigeons and the interpretive dance.

"We begin," he said, grandly unfurling a napkin, "with candles. Soft accordion music. Perhaps some poetry readings. Bilingual, of course. Culture is nothing without confusion."

Maria narrowed her eyes. "In French?"

"*Mais oui!*"

George coughed directly into his feta. Theodora, without looking up from peeling garlic, muttered a prayer.

"And the menu," Claude said, voice rising like the overture to a particularly ambitious opera, "shall reflect our two noble cuisines. Greek soul... with a French twist."

There was a beat.

Then Alex, speaking very slowly, the way one does to someone holding scissors and just enough enthusiasm to be dangerous, asked, "And what exactly would that entail?"

Claude beamed. "I've already spoken to Dimitri. We shall serve... frogs' legs."

A pause.

A long one.

A breeze passed. Somewhere, a cat hissed. The cicadas gave up.

"You want to cook *frogs*?" Theodora asked, as if double-checking she hadn't misheard a crime being committed.

"Delicately!" Claude nodded, mistaking her tone entirely. "In lemon butter! *Très élégant!*"

Theodora crossed herself twice.

"You're talking about the noisy swamp creatures that show up during rain?" asked George.

"They're a plague," Claude said. "We have plenty! And the French have turned them into a delicacy. Art from aquatic abundance!"

"They're not food," snapped Theodora. "They're noise with legs."

Claude's face lit up like it was Christmas and Bastille Day rolled into one. "Exactly! That's French cuisine!"

And with that, the village spiralled into a full-blown ethical, culinary, and amphibious crisis.

The Legend of the Frog-Eating Foreigners had never been heard of before. The idea, not only of not disliking them and not dodging them during mating season, but of actually cooking and consuming them, struck the village like a thunderclap.

Oh, there were whispers. A rumour passed down by a sailor who once claimed, over a suspiciously strong ouzo, that he'd visited a land where people willingly dined on frogs.

"They put them on plates," he'd slurred, "like fish. But uglier. They say it's elegant. I say it's witchcraft."

No one had believed him. Because why would they? Frogs were things you dodged on dark roads. Creatures that ruined weddings by croaking through the vows. No one actually ate them. That was like chewing on a locust and calling it tapas.

And now Claude – linen-wrapped, accordion-humming Claude – wanted to serve them at *Zorba's*?

Maria went on the offensive. "I will call the papers," she announced. "The real ones. With scandals." A few minutes later, she was also spreading a rumour that Claude intended to recite poetry about frogs during dinner.

Eleni suggested filing a municipal petition under the category of Culinary Threats, and warned that serving frogs could upset the ecological balance and possibly the church choir.

Dimitri, who had initially agreed mostly because Claude promised him free wine, backed out dramatically after catching one and being stared down by it.

"I saw myself in its eyes," he whispered. "And I didn't like what I saw."

Even Spiros weighed in, declaring from his bench that the frogs had "done nothing wrong", and if Claude served them, "there'd be consequences. And not just gastronomic ones."

He later muttered that in his day, if someone served frogs, it was considered a declaration of war. Possibly on France.

As word spread through the village, opinions multiplied like… well, frogs.

Some were cautiously intrigued. Most were deeply offended.

Even Father Evangelos, when approached for a blessing, simply raised his eyebrows and whispered, "Let him try."

Theodora, however, was not whispering.

"If he puts frogs on my *stove*," she announced, "I will sauté *him* in lemon and garlic."

Claude insisted on hosting a pre-event "philosophical symposium" under the lemon trees.

He called it "From Amphibian to Ambrosia: A Culinary Dialogue".

Five spectators showed up. One was Katerina. Claude wore a black turtleneck. In July.

He read aloud from Camus. He quoted Voltaire. He tried to draw a parallel between Zeus and French cheese.

Theodora arrived halfway through, carrying a pan and a wooden spoon like a battle drum.

"If I hear the word 'fusion' one more time," she said, "I will fuse your accordion with your head."

Claude hung his head gravely. "You reject the modern."

"I reject frogs," she snapped.

Maria declared this the best theatre the village had seen since the electricity cut during last year's nativity play.

The night before the event, tragedy struck.

Claude's accordion, a battered but beloved instrument that had serenaded many a confused tourist, disappeared.

Vanished. Gone.

Claude was devastated. "They've censored my soul!"

Rumours flew. Dimitri claimed Katerina had eaten it. George suggested it had fled voluntarily. Theodora said nothing but was later seen polishing her best ladle.

Claude tried to proceed with the evening using a tambourine and a Spotify playlist titled *"Mélancholie sous la lune"*.

It was... not a success.

On the night of the Great Cultural Fusion, the taverna was full. Mostly out of morbid curiosity. Claude's first dish was served: small plates with two very dainty, very greenish frog legs, garnished with dill and poetic suffering.

Dimitri tried one, blinked twice, and asked if it was revenge for something he didn't remember doing. No one else ate them. George sniffed and went back to his bread.

Theodora dramatically unveiled her own counter-offensive: roasted lamb, lemon potatoes, *spanakopita*, and a dish called "Real Food, Thank You Very Much". The crowd erupted in cheers.

Claude wept into his scarf. He conceded defeat with grace. Sort of.

He agreed to never serve frogs again. In exchange, Theodora allowed him one "French Night" per year, under strict supervision and only if the accordion never returned and there were no frogs.

Maria wrote a full account of the scandal for her "Zorba's Digest" newsletter.

Claude, licking his wounds (and possibly a leftover olive tapenade), raised a toast. "To tradition and innovation. And to never trusting a Greek grandmother's stove."

And Zorba, sitting in his usual chair, finally spoke. "No frogs. No fusion. Just food." Everyone agreed. Even Claude.

Katerina burped in approval.

CHAPTER FORTY-TWO

MARMITE AND MAYHEM

It began with a thud at the front gate and a cardboard box wrapped in enough brown tape to tranquillise a goat.

I eyed it suspiciously.

Alex leaned over my shoulder. "Is it ticking?"

"It's from England," I said, as though that were an answer.

"Ah," she replied. "So yes, then."

The label said "Emergency supplies".

We opened it with a kitchen knife and a sense of impending doom.

Inside were four packets of Yorkshire Tea (so strong it could summon ghosts), ten jars of Marmite, a beige woollen cardigan, and a handwritten note from my sister that read:

"Thought you might be missing the taste of home.
P.S. I knitted the cardigan.
P.P.S. Hope Greece isn't *too* sunny."

It was 34°C in the shade. The cardigan started sweating immediately.

Alex held it up like it had bitten her. "You'll melt," she said.

"It's emotional insulation," I replied.

The Marmite was placed reverently on the bar. Within an hour, half the village had gathered like archaeologists around a cursed relic. George squinted at the label. "Is this for engines?"

"It's yeast extract," I said.

"Like... for making bread?"

"More like if bread had a midlife crisis and reinvented itself as an alien."

My sister assumed that all Brits abroad miss something.

For some, it's proper tea. For others, tinned baked beans, decent chocolate, or the specific misery of a soggy British biscuit. For my sister, she would always miss Marmite, so naturally, she assumed I felt the same.

And she was right. Who wouldn't?

Marmite tastes like home.

Like toast in a cold kitchen. Like being five years old and slightly confused about breakfast. Like something that dares you not to like it, and usually wins.

But ten jars, wrapped in a cardigan and love. I certainly would never miss it again.

Claude, naturally, insisted on tasting it. He dipped a finger in, raised it to his lips with tragic dignity, and immediately collapsed into a chair.

"This," he gasped, "is what philosophy tastes like when it gives up."

Maria crossed herself. "It smells like Dimitri's shoes," she muttered.

Dimitri sniffed the jar, took a step back and said, "I've eaten a fermented otter. This is worse."

Theodora squinted into the jar. "It smells like something that came out of a haunted toaster." She tried cleaning a burnt pot with it. "It doesn't come off," she said. "Whatever this is, it's now part of the pan."

Then Katerina trotted up. She sniffed the Marmite, licked an entire toast slice clean, blinked, burped, and then headbutted the bench.

"She likes it," Claude whispered.

"She once ate a broom handle," said Alex.

"She has taste," said Claude.

"She once ate my tax returns," said Eleni.

Claude, flushed with Marmite-induced euphoria, declared it deserved reverence.

"It is an acquired taste," he said. "Like Dimitri's *tsipouro*, or George's wine."

Maria, already halfway through her second scandal of the day, clapped her hands. "We must decide this properly." Everyone groaned. "A contest," she added. Groans intensified. "A taste-off. Marmite vs. ouzo."

Dimitri grinned. "Let's do it."

Alex sighed. "Do we have insurance?"

No one answered.

Two tables were set up for the Marmite vs. Ouzo Showdown. One labelled "**MARMITE**", decorated with a tiny British flag someone coloured with crayon. One labelled "**OUZO**", surrounded by olives, and Theodora sharpening her glare.

There would be three rounds.

Villagers would taste both, then cast a vote. Not for what they *liked*, but for what they *survived*.

Vassiliki took a bite of Marmite toast with the solemnity of a woman entering a tomb.

She chewed. She paused. She shot back a glass of ouzo.

"The Marmite tastes like boiled socks," she said. "But now I don't care."

Dimitri spooned it directly into his mouth, drank ouzo, and whispered, "I saw my ancestors. They were frowning."

Claude cried. "It's beautiful. Like despair… with vitamins."

Spiros, under pressure and lacking cigarettes, licked Marmite off a knife, drank ouzo, and immediately fell asleep.

Next, the village children, sensing mischief and sugar-free treats, begged to take part in the Marmite tasting. But it was agreed, no ouzo for anyone under twelve. Alex, against her better judgement, agreed, provided she supervised and no one caught fire.

Within minutes, it was clear this had been a terrible decision.

One child smeared Marmite on his forearm and pronounced himself invisible. Another tried to swap a slice of toast for someone's flip-flops, claiming they were now "cursed with Britishness". A third swore he could hear Big Ben chime.

Then one small boy dipped a biscuit into the ouzo (despite the no-ouzo-for-under-12s rule), took a thoughtful bite, and announced it was "better than Grandma's soup". His grandmother quietly left, with her ladle, and no intention of forgiving him.

Round three became known as The Philosophical Collapse. Claude recited a haiku:

Dark spread, ancient rage,
Yeast beneath a morning sun–
My tongue mourns itself.

Maria, dressed in sunglasses and a fake British accent, attempted to broadcast "live radio" from the event using a wooden spoon as a microphone.

Eleni tried to file a petition to have Marmite declared a controlled substance.

Katerina broke into the Marmite stash and ate the contents of an entire jar. Nobody asked how she got the lid off. Nobody really cared. It was just one less jar to worry about. "She's possessed," Maria whispered.

Zorba watched silently. He stood and walked to the Marmite. He dipped a finger in the jar and tasted it. He paused, looked at the sea, and said, "I have questions about the British." He drank ouzo and sat down. That was his verdict.

Votes were cast using olive pits: simple, elegant, flawed.

- Marmite: 6 votes (1 Claude, 1 lost tourist, 2 children, 1 goat, 1 pity vote from someone who didn't understand the question)
- Ouzo: 51 votes
- One olive pit found in a child's ear (counted as abstaining)

The Marmite was resealed, wrapped in cling film, labelled "For emergency use only", and stored next to Dimitri's most dangerous *tsipouro*.

Katerina was seen licking a paper plate after lapping a glass of ouzo with an expression of smug satisfaction.

Maria began planning a British baked bean tasting.

Alex said if anyone posted photos of the event, she would change her name and move to Iceland.

And me? I just wrote it all down. Because in this village, even the strangest things – a black British spread, a drunken goat, and a spoonful of misplaced loyalty – can become part of our story.

And in the end, that's what we do. We argue. We taste. We survive. We remember.

And, occasionally, we burp Marmite.

CHAPTER FORTY-THREE

How to Start a Religious Schism with a Teabag

I n Greece, tea is not a drink.

It's a diagnosis.

You're given tea when your soul is unwell, your blood is weak, or your mother has decided you look "a bit pale". Tea is what grandmothers make when they're too worried to make soup. It's medicine. It's punishment. It is never, under any circumstances, consumed by the healthy.

Coffee, on the other hand, is the national bloodstream. It is brewed thick as treacle, stirred with philosophy and cigarette ash, and taken five times a day by people who insist they're "cutting back".

So when I brought out the box of Yorkshire Tea, retrieved reverently from the English care package, the villagers approached like it might contain cursed scrolls. "It's a special blend," I said. "Very British. Strong. Bold. Restorative."

Alex offered to make it properly. The full performance.

She boiled the kettle, selected a teapot, and prepared it the way generations of British matrons would expect: hot, black, tannic, and blessed with a splash of milk.

Maria watched from the doorway with arms folded and eyes narrowed like a priest spotting sacrilege.

"You boil the water?" she asked cautiously.

"Yes."

"Then pour it... on the tea bags?"

"That's right."

She frowned.

"And then... *milk*?"

"Correct."

Maria crossed herself, mumbled something about "culinary blasphemy", and went to find Theodora.

Claude took the first sip. He swirled it thoughtfully, then announced, "It tastes like mud in a rainstorm."

Spiros sniffed it, added a splash of *tsipouro*, and declared it "almost passable if you close one eye and pretend it's something else".

Dimitri took his cup, poured it over ice, added honey and lime juice, then handed it to a nearby tourist with a flourish.

"Try this," he said. "It's the Anglo–Greek Gut Purifier. Good for digestion, emotional clarity, and confusing Germans."

The tourist loved it, and asked for two more. Dimitri started designing labels.

Things went downhill from there.

George tried a sip, said nothing, then silently spread butter on his toast using the teabag.

Theodora appeared just in time to see Claude pouring another cup.

"You drink that," she warned, "and I'll ban you from the kitchen for a week."

"It's cultural exchange," Claude insisted. "We must explore flavour! Challenge the senses!"

"Challenge your senses with garlic and a frying pan," she replied.

Maria, who had taken a teaspoonful for testing purposes, declared it "the taste equivalent of being left by your husband during Lent". Then she made herself a Greek coffee and glared at everyone for the next hour.

Katerina, as ever, was undeterred. She trotted up to the table, stuck her nose into an abandoned teacup, licked once, and sneezed violently. Then she headbutted the milk jug and walked off, offended.

The division was immediate. Unlike with the Marmite, we

hadn't asked people to vote, but a brief and unofficial referendum was still held in the bakery queue. The results:

- **Pro-Tea:** 4 votes (Alex, me, Claude – under protest – and a passing hiker from Bristol)
- **Anti-Tea:** 36 votes (everyone else, including the baker's wife, who hadn't even tried it but "didn't like the sound of it")
- **Undecided:** 1 goat (Katerina later chewed the cardboard box the tea came in, which some took as support)

Afterwards, Maria began referring to it as *the incident*.

Eleni added "boiling dairy beverages" to her growing list of prohibited activities within municipal zones.

Theodora threatened to confiscate the kettle unless it was used exclusively for "legitimate herbal infusions", i.e. mountain tea, chamomile, and anything that could plausibly be harvested during a pilgrimage.

Claude returned to his wine and olives, claiming he'd suffered "a brief period of imperialist disorientation".

Dimitri sold four more "Gut Purifiers" and began experimenting with Marmite-iced *tsipouro*, which we warned him might violate the Geneva Convention.

Alex just smiled and made herself another cup.

As for me, I sat in the shade, holding a mug of strong, milky, deeply misunderstood Yorkshire Tea. I took a sip, listened to the birds, and tried not to take it personally when the village stared like I'd just eaten a boiled frog in church.

Because sometimes, cultural exchange isn't about understanding. It's about knowing when to offer the first cup. And when to quietly make another for yourself.

Later that evening, I made the mistake of wearing the cardigan to the taverna.

Within five minutes, I had sweated through both the cardigan and the chair, a passing German couple had asked if I was feeling unwell, and Eleni had offered me a hot-water bottle, "just in case".

Claude said I looked like "an English ghost lost in a Mediterranean dream".

Zorba nodded solemnly and handed me a double *tsipouro*. "To dull the pain," he said.

Alex confiscated the cardigan and used it to dry glasses.

Eventually, the cardigan was repurposed as a goat blanket. The Marmite now sits proudly in the back pantry, out of Katerina's reach.

And the tea? Alex still makes it occasionally, and brings it to me when the wind shifts and I get that faraway look in my eyes that says I'm briefly homesick.

She never says anything. She just hands me the mug. And for a moment, I'm in two places at once. Beneath the olive trees, but also in a rainy English kitchen with the smell of toast and carpet shampoo.

Then I sip, and remember:

I came here for the sun.

I stayed for the havoc.

But I'll always drink the tea.

CHAPTER FORTY-FOUR

ALEX'S AUNT FROM ATHENS

Every Greek family has one. The aunt – the *Thea*. The immovable force of maternal authority, wrapped in Chanel No. 5 and opinions sharp enough to peel a lemon.

For Alex, that woman was Aunt Despina.

She didn't arrive. She descended.

Her text came two days before, short and clear as a court summons: "I will visit. You need supervision. Prepare." We didn't know what for, but we prepared anyway.

Despina stepped off the coach like it was a red carpet. Her hair was perfect. Her bag was monogrammed. Her sunglasses were so large they may have been used for picking up Wi-Fi signals.

She paused. She looked around the square. She tilted her head like a critic inspecting a half-finished museum exhibit.

Alex beamed. "Aunt Despina, welcome!"

"Why is the goat staring at me?" she asked, nodding towards Katerina, who was lounging near the flowerpots.

"She lives here," I said.

Despina pursed her lips. "So do weeds."

Despina surveyed the taverna. She tutted, softly, but with intent. We braced ourselves.

Just as Despina was about to begin her critique, a new force entered from the lemon grove:

Mana. Theodora's mother. Our resident oracle, supervisor, unsolicited commentator, and undisputed queen of the stool near the kitchen door, in her traditional all-black outfit.

She carried a wooden spoon like a sceptre and surveyed the taverna like it belonged to her, which, in a spiritual sense, it probably did. Her gaze locked with Despina's across the room like two retired generals meeting on neutral ground.

No words. Just a slow, solemn nod from both.

Maria whispered, "Oh no. We've reached critical matriarch."

Despina went for aesthetics. Mana was there for order.

Despina criticised the curtains, rearranged the lemons for better visual symmetry, and declared Claude's scarf "a cry for attention".

Mana lifted each saucepan lid and sniffed, then inspected the mop.

It was a standoff. Two titans. Two queens. One taverna.

And then, like magic, they began to agree. The breakthrough came with the *tzatziki*.

Despina reached for the dill. Mana shook her head. "Not too much." Despina paused. Then nodded. And they stirred the bowl *together*.

The goat sneezed. The air shifted. Something had changed.

Within the hour, the two women were gossiping like long-lost cousins reunited at a funeral.

They compared recipes. They insulted Theodora's fridge organisation. They briefly touched on politics, agreed it was hopeless, and returned to criticising the menu.

Alex watched it all with a mix of pride and dread. "We're not in charge any more, are we?" she whispered.

"No," I said. "We're witnesses."

Theodora had taken the day off. It was meant to be calm. It wasn't.

By 10:00, Despina and Mana were in the kitchen.

By 10:05, they had rewritten the entire menu.

Mana made meatballs with mint. Despina made a *pastitsio* that resembled a Byzantine palace.

Claude suggested a French twist. Despina told him to go twist somewhere else.

Spiros sat outside, blinking at the sky and muttering, "There are too many powerful women in this village."

George agreed, quietly. He held his cheese like perhaps it might protect him.

The food was wonderful.

Zorba actually complimented something without swearing. Father Evangelos blessed the roast lamb twice – just in case. Even Katerina stayed away from the kitchen. Out of respect. Or fear.

By nightfall, Despina and Mana were sipping *retsina* under the olive tree, arms crossed, watching the rest of us scurry around like servants in their private kingdom.

They toasted. Despina raised her glass. "To stubborn women."

Mana clinked hers. "And good pans."

The next morning, Despina packed her bags with clinical precision – the kind that suggested she'd done this before, possibly in wartime.

"Your father still can't work the microwave," she reminded Alex. "If I don't check in, he'll try to steam a *tiropita* again."

"You could stay," Alex offered. "We've got a spare room."

"Don't be ridiculous," Despina said, kissing her cheek. "I love you. But if I stay any longer, I'll end up reorganising the stockroom and accidentally owning the lease."

She turned to Mana. The two women nodded once, firmly.

"I'll send you the recipe for the stuffing," Despina said.

"And I'll send you a real wooden spoon," Mana replied.

That, in Greek terms, was a formal pact of sisterhood.

She left nothing behind but the faint scent of expensive soap, a perfectly alphabetised spice rack, and a warning that she'd be back "when standards begin to slip".

Mana's stool now had a new cushion.

Despina had placed it there, claiming the stool looked uncomfortable.

Mana insisted it had been her idea all along.

We didn't argue. The cushion stayed.

The kitchen is now unofficially run by a rotating committee of strong women, one goat, and whichever grandchild is most recently out of favour.

"I always thought they'd hate each other," Alex said.

I looked out at Mana muttering into the soup and Katerina licking a lemon.

"They still might," I said. "But now they'll do it over coffee."

A note on aunts: some people arrive and change your life. Despina arrived, reorganised the spice rack, critiqued our taverna philosophy, terrified our staff, and somehow made everything better.

We haven't seen her since. But the lemon grove still smells faintly of her perfume.

And the meat, somehow, tastes… wiser.

CHAPTER FORTY-FIVE

ZORBA'S DREAM

Zorba doesn't say much.

He prefers grunting, sipping, and raising one eyebrow in a way that makes you question your entire life's decisions.

But every so often, when the moon is full and the *tsipouro* is flowing, he talks.

And on this particular evening, as the crickets tuned up their nighttime orchestra and the sea made its slow, shushing argument with the sand, Zorba spoke. "I had a dream," he said, between sips. "A big one."

That got our attention. Zorba doesn't usually dream. Or if he does, he doesn't tell anyone unless it involves fishing quotas or expired ouzo.

"Go on," Alex said, cautious.

"In my dream," Zorba said, leaning back in his chair, "I was in the taverna. But it wasn't a taverna. It was… a school."

"A school?" Claude perked up, already reaching for a pen. "Like a Platonic academy?"

"Exactly," Zorba nodded. "Except with better chairs. And everyone was drinking. But respectfully."

He explained that in the dream, Plato was sitting under the lemon tree, writing on a napkin. Socrates was at the bar, arguing with Katerina. A lemon flew across the sky, trailing olive oil and flaming feta. The menu had no prices, just quotes. You could pay in wisdom or fish. Maria ran a booth called "Rumours & Rhetoric" and was doing brisk business.

"And then," Zorba said solemnly, "someone shouted, 'Let the debate begin!' And suddenly, everyone stood on the tables and started shouting about destiny and parking."

"Sounds like Tuesday," George muttered.

Claude took this as divine inspiration. "We must host a debate night," he said, eyes aglow. "An open forum of philosophical exchange. Zorba's Dream: The Symposium!"

"No," said Alex.

"Yes," said Claude. And so, inevitably… we did.

Zorba's Parthenon - A Taverna by the Sea

It was advertised on a single handwritten poster stuck to the door:

ZORBA'S DREAM:
An Evening of Intellectual Ferment & Local Cheese

Bring thoughts. And a chair.

Theodora made *spanakopita*. Dimitri made a batch of experimental lemon *tsipouro*. Claude wore a toga. Unironically.

At first, it was civil. Claude opened with a reading from Camus. Spiros responded by coughing loudly and muttering, "Get to the good bit."

Maria posed the evening's first question: "Is gossip a form of truth, or merely its rehearsal?"

This prompted a twenty-minute argument between two fishermen and a man who hadn't spoken since 2003. Then Katerina entered, and everything unravelled.

She strode in like she owned the place, which, philosophically, she may. She climbed the stage (a crate). She ate Claude's quote cards, headbutted the microphone, and then, in a gesture that felt deeply symbolic, she knocked over the "Free Thinking" chalkboard and lay down beside it.

"She's making a statement," Claude whispered.

"She's making a mess," said Alex.

Theodora tried to shoo her away with a mop. She stole the mop and refused to return it.

George delivered an impassioned monologue on feta as a metaphor for human fragility. Dimitri challenged Claude to a logic duel involving boiled octopus. A tourist asked what the topic was and was met with silence.

Father Evangelos blessed the stage, the goat, and the mop.

And through it all, Zorba watched, silent, sipping, a small smile tugging at the corners of his mouth.

Eventually, as with all things Greek, the debate gave way to dancing. Maria declared herself the winner of the evening. No one disagreed. Claude tried to launch "Zorba's School of Thought" as a weekly event. Alex banned it immediately. Katerina ate the suggestion box.

The next morning, the only evidence of the Great Symposium was a lemon in the fig tree, a philosophy quote chalked on the toilet door ("I think, therefore I drink"), and a lingering sense that something important had almost happened.

Zorba arrived, as usual, at 11 a.m.

He looked around, sat down, and sipped his *tsipouro*.

Then he said, "I liked the flying lemon."

To be fair, the lemon had sailed across the courtyard during a heated debate about vinegar ratios, bounced once off a chair, and landed neatly in the fig tree.

"More tavernas need flying lemons," he said.

And that, we all agreed, was probably true.

CHAPTER FORTY-SIX

THE OFFER

It happened quietly, like most dangerous things do. No fanfare. No meeting. No printed plans. Just a sleek silver car that rolled into the village one Thursday afternoon, too polished, too clean, too *Athens*.

It didn't park, it *posed*, beneath the olive tree outside the *kafenio*, its glossy finish reflecting the sea as if it had arrived not to visit, but to conquer.

Two men stepped out of the car.

One wore shoes that had clearly never touched a field. The other carried a leather folder that had never been within five metres of oregano.

They looked like they'd been printed from the same glossy brochure. Even their sunglasses seemed unnaturally un-smeared.

They wanted Zorba.

Not Alex, not the mayor, not the cooperative. Only Zorba.

It didn't take long to realise these weren't the same two as before; they were the next level up. The serious ones.

The first pair had been the advanced party: polite, curious, vaguely threatening in a bureaucratic sort of way.

These two had come with plans. Spreadsheets. Renderings.

They spoke of "heritage opportunity zones".

Of curated experiences.

Of a "sanitised traditional Greek village", with optional spa upgrades, multilingual audio guides, and a daily olive-picking demonstration performed by an actor named Stavros who, in real life, worked in marketing.

They had a vision. Cobbled streets with hidden drainage. A souvenir shop shaped like a fishing boat, but selling nothing a fisherman would ever use. A taverna that served "authentic Greek cuisine" with meat-free moussaka and a QR-code menu. Everything freshly painted in regulation white, with just the right amount of artificial weathering for Instagram.

Zorba was sitting exactly where you'd expect him: beneath the rusted tin awning at the side of the taverna, nursing a thick coffee and staring at the sea like it had offended him.

They joined him, uninvited, sitting at his table. They

ordered nothing. No one heard what was said, not exactly.

But Maria's second cousin saw them lean in. Saw the man in the suit unzip the folder. Saw Zorba lean back in that way he does when he's halfway between amused and murderous. Fifteen minutes later, the silver car was gone.

Something had changed.

Zorba didn't say anything. Not that day. Not the next. He showed up to the taverna as usual. He drank his coffee. He grunted at the world. But he didn't sit in the grove. He didn't glance at the trees.

And when Claude asked if he'd heard the rumour about the "eco-villas", Zorba simply said, "People hear many things. Most of them are wrong." Which, in village terms, meant *something was definitely right.*

Alex heard it from Spiros, who claimed the man in the silver car didn't blink once during the entire meeting, "like a lizard, but more expensive". She stood still for a long moment, then walked behind the taverna and stood among the lemon trees.

She stayed there for over an hour, not gardening, not cleaning, just… thinking.

I found her eventually, fingers resting lightly on one of the lower branches.

"They're trying to buy it," she said.

Later, quietly, Zorba told me, over a drink, at sunset. Like men confessing crimes or admitting they once danced badly in public.

"They offered good money," he said. "For the taverna, and the lemon grove."

"How much?"

He shrugged. "Enough."

"And?"

He looked at me, eyes unreadable beneath the brim of his salt-stained cap.

"They're still circling," he said. "Want to build something. Tidy. Branded. The kind of place with brochures in six languages and background music you can't turn off."

We'd heard it before, from men with folders and polished shoes, promising progress and politely asking where to put the souvenir shop. They used words like *enhancement* and *experience*.

"They said it would bring jobs. Visitors. Opportunity."

He paused.

Then added, "No one asked me if I *wanted* to sell. They just assumed I hadn't thought of it yet."

I nodded slowly. "And did you?"

He looked out at the trees, his eyes narrowing slightly as the breeze rustled through the leaves.

"I thought about it," he said.

Zorba hadn't said yes. But he hadn't said no either. And in a Greek village, that kind of silence creates more tension than a thunderstorm over a plastic pergola. It was a pause. A warning. Or the moment before something begins.

It was all anyone could talk about, quietly, carefully, usually while pretending to talk about something else.

"Nice lemons this year," Theodora said, while chopping onions with unnecessary force.

"Very round," agreed Maria. "Almost... irreplaceable."

Even Claude, usually lost in the haze of philosophical detachment and overlong vowels, had stopped quoting Camus for a full twenty-four hours.

The grove felt different now. Like it was watching. Waiting.

So was Alex. Until one morning, she stopped waiting.

"It's not a protest," she said, tying her hair back with the sort of determination that usually meant someone was about to repaint the house or move all the furniture.

"It looks like a protest," I said, eyeing the hand-painted sign she was holding.

"Lemon Day. Open to all," it said.

"It's not a protest," she replied. "It's a celebration."

"Of what?"

"Of the grove. Of the people who love it. Of what it's *for*."

"And if Zorba comes?"

She grinned. "Then we'll make him some lemonade."

The Lemon Day began as a "community harvest". Nothing formal. Just word of mouth, a few baskets, and Maria telling absolutely everyone within earshot.

By mid-morning, the grove was full. Children ran between the trees with sticky fingers and lemon peels. Dimitri grilled sardines on a home-made barbeque that looked like it had been welded together by chance. Theodora brought lemon pies. Vassiliki brought a cake so intense it caused a short argument about legal sugar limits.

Claude played music – actual music, not existential fusion – and somehow got a small group of tourists to join a traditional dance that started as a circle and ended as a mess.

People laughed. They picked lemons. They swapped stories about Zorba's uncle, about who once climbed which tree, about which lemon had healed which ailment. Someone swore they'd met their spouse under that very branch. Someone else said the branch used to belong to another tree entirely.

Nobody cared.

It was a day for remembering.

And for showing.

Alex didn't stand up and give a speech. She didn't need to. She just made sure every child who picked a lemon took one home. She made sure Spiros had a chair in the shade. She walked past Zorba's usual table, placed a slice of pie beside his empty coffee cup, and left without a word.

At first, Zorba just sat on the bench above the path, the one that overlooked the lemon trees, like a captain watching a storm he hadn't decided whether to sail into.

He saw Eleni hand out jars of home-made jam, each one labelled "Property of no one, for use by all".

He saw George show a little boy how to plant wild oregano by the fence.

He saw Maria refuse to let anyone throw away the peels. "For the marmalade! For the soap! For the soul of the grove!"

And then he saw Alex. Laughing. Wiping flour off her dress. Balancing a tray of lemonade glasses like she'd been born doing it.

She looked up at him and smiled.

Zorba didn't smile back, but he didn't look away either.

That evening, long after the crowd had wandered home full and sun-dazed, Alex and I stood in the grove alone. The wind had quieted. The air still smelled of citrus, charcoal.

"You think it worked?" I asked.

Alex didn't answer straight away.

Instead, she knelt and picked a fallen lemon from the grass. One that had split in the sun.

It wasn't the polished, imported kind that sits under fluorescent lights pretending to be sunshine. This one had been grown under real sun, the kind that makes paint fade and old men nap.

Its skin was thick, dimpled, and uneven, like it had lived a little. Still clinging to the scent of the grove, of hot leaves and honeyed air. As Alex peeled it back it released a sigh, sharp, floral, and immediate, the kind of scent that made you stand up straighter.

The juice shimmered with gold and memory, sticky on your fingers, impossible to forget. It didn't just taste sour; it tasted alive.

Greek lemons aren't perfect. They're better than perfect. They're real.

"I don't want to fight him," she said. "I just want him to remember what this place is worth."

Then she handed me the lemon. It was warm. Imperfect. And maybe more powerful than anything in a folder with a logo.

CHAPTER FORTY-SEVEN

WHY IS THE GOAT WEARING A BADGE?

We were still waiting. Waiting for Zorba's answer. Waiting to find out if everything we'd built, the taverna, the grove, the carefully balanced mayhem of our Greek experiment, was about to be paved over or politely replaced by something with a helipad.

And, while we waited, the universe sent us a distraction. A flaming one. Or at least, one wearing a uniform and shiny shoes.

It began with an aura of bureaucracy so strong it parted the oregano.

A man stood at the taverna gate. Navy shirt. Sunglasses that reflected judgment. A fire department badge that glinted ominously in the sun.

"I am Officer Panagiotis," he announced. "Municipal Fire Safety Division."

Everyone froze.

Maria dropped a basket of cutlery. Claude froze mid-poem. Theodora swore at an aubergine.

"I am here," Officer Panagiotis continued, "for a random inspection and compulsory live fire drill."

Alex blinked. "A drill?"

"Effective immediately," he said, consulting a form that may or may not have been summoning spirits.

"Can we reschedule?" I asked, foolishly.

"No," he replied. "This is Greece. There are no appointments. Only consequences."

Eleni, already red in the face from a morning of municipality forms, started complaining about Article 4, Section C of the National Tavern Emergency Response Code and threatened to file a letter protesting the surprise of it all. To whom, she wouldn't say.

Claude, who had only just sat down with his morning wine, stood up and declared: "Let us make this a performance! A fiery ballet of bureaucracy and flame!"

"No flames!" Alex snapped.

"Symbolic flames!" Claude amended.

Dimitri asked, quite seriously, whether it would help if he set fire to the old fridge.

"Absolutely not," Alex growled. "We're trying to pass the inspection, not summon the coastguard."

Katerina wandered up to the officer, sniffed his clipboard, and gently chewed one corner before trotting away with the calm assurance of someone who had seen worse.

Officer Panagiotis surveyed the scene like a military general confronted with a theatre troupe. He produced a stopwatch.

"You have ten minutes to prepare. I will observe from a neutral zone."

He pointed to Spiros's bench.

"No," said Spiros, who was currently sitting on Spiros's bench. "This is not a neutral zone. This is my bench."

The officer nodded, impressed. "Understood." He moved to the olive tree.

Meanwhile, Claude had begun crafting an evacuation plan on a napkin using ketchup and dramatic arrows. Theodora fashioned a makeshift siren out of two pot lids. Maria declared herself "Chief Alarm" and began warming up her vocal cords like a soprano preparing for opening night, preferably in a production where the set catches fire, someone faints in Act Two, and no one is entirely sure if it's still a comedy.

George quietly moved all the cheese to the beach.

"Why?" I asked.

"In case it melts," he said.

Alex took one look at the chaos and sighed. "Fine. Let's burn metaphorically."

At exactly 12:30, Maria shrieked, "FIRE!"

A tourist applauded. "Oh! An immersive cultural activity!"

The Belgian couple asked if they could eat while evacuating.

Theodora banged her pans. Claude began narrating the drill in broken Greek and interpretive mime. Dimitri ran out the back door, shouting something about protecting the bees.

Eleni attempted to direct foot traffic with a flowchart and a rolled-up tax form. She got into a heated argument with a passing cat.

Father Evangelos, in full robes and oven mitts, stood near the wine rack and calmly began blessing everything within reach, including the extinguisher, a pepper grinder, and a very startled Swedish tourist.

Katerina trotted into the kitchen, climbed onto a chair like she owned the place, and headbutted the emergency fire escape map off the wall.

Officer Panagiotis stood under the olive tree, inscrutable, and made notes on a carbon triplicate form.

"Is this a theme event?" asked an American woman.

"It's very real," Alex said. "Tragically."

Claude passed out leaflets he'd just written titled "Flame and Fate: A Poetic Response to Public Safety".

One child asked if they could pet the goat.

A man from Thessaloniki live-streamed the entire drill and commented: "Come for the seafood, stay for the evacuation."

It ended with Maria collapsing from exhaustion, Claude slipping on spilled *tzatziki*, Theodora interrupting the drill to announce the *moussaka* was getting cold, Katerina sleeping on the fire extinguisher wearing Officer Panagiotis's badge, and Spiros, perfectly still, declaring, "I survived the Junta; I can survive this." Officer Panagiotis stepped forward.

He looked at his notes, then at the smouldering dignity of Zorba's.

"There is room for improvement," he said.

"Is that an official rating?" Alex asked.

"No," he replied. "That's just being kind."

Then he left. No fine. No compliment. Just a small nod. And a whispered, "May your extinguisher never be tested."

Celebratory shots of *tsipouro* and extra *pastitsio* for anyone who'd moved more than three metres during the drill marked the end. Maria started planning next month's, while Claude suggested mood music. Dimitri declared, "I'll bring flares!" Alex guzzled wine straight from the bottle. Spiros, finally rising, stretched and said, "If the goat gets a badge, I deserve a medal." So we gave him one – an Alpha beer bottle cap. He wore it all week.

The next day, a suspicious silence fell over the taverna. That meant only one thing: Eleni was writing something.

She had commandeered Table Three, the one closest to the lemon grove and furthest from Spiros's bench, as she said he interfered with her concentration. A large folder sat beside her, filled with regulatory forms, colour-coded tabs, and a stapler that had seen war. She was hunched over a legal pad, talking to herself.

I asked cautiously, "Everything alright?"

She didn't look up. "I'm filing a formal response."

"To what?"

"To the absurdity," she said.

Maria leaned in. "Is it about Claude setting off the extinguisher in the basil plant again?"

"No," Eleni snapped. "That was… expected. This is about the inspection. The officer's attitude. The procedural vagueness. The goat slander."

"Did he insult the goat?" I asked.

"He implied she was combustible."

Katerina, asleep under the table with a paper napkin in her mouth, sneezed in protest.

Officer Panagiotis's unexpected arrival – clipboard in one hand, fire extinguisher checklist in the other – shook things up. He came for a fire safety inspection, but stayed long enough to question our electrical wiring, our exit strategy, and whether *tsipouro* counted as an accelerant.

It was the kind of bureaucratic theatre that briefly took over everyone's attention.

But beneath the flurry of forms and Dimitri trying to argue that "fire is a state of mind", the real question still smouldered.

Would Zorba sell the taverna?

None of us said it out loud. But the worry was there – flickering quietly, just like the wiring Panagiotis had warned us about. Meanwhile, we waited. We waited for Zorba.

Chapter Forty-Eight

Zorba's Answer

Zorba didn't come to the taverna for two weeks after Lemon Day.

In Telios terms, that was the equivalent of the Parthenon taking a week off – and threatening to list itself on Airbnb.

We were all worried about him. But, if we're honest, we were even more worried about ourselves. Was he really going to sell everything from under us?

His coffee cup sat untouched on its usual table. His bench under the tin roof remained unclaimed, except by one bold chicken who was swiftly removed by Dimitri (and then argued with him for ten minutes). The sea continued to exist, but without Zorba staring at it, it seemed... less certain.

Nobody mentioned it. Which, of course, meant everyone was talking about it.

"I think he's angry," Maria said, folding napkins aggressively.

"He's thinking," said Eleni, as if she had intimate access to his inner monologue.

"He's building suspense," added Claude, stroking his chin like a theatre critic.

Alex just kept working. Wiping down tables, trimming the oregano patch, walking the grove in slow, deliberate loops.

"He'll come when he's ready," she said.

And, of course, he did, eventually.

It was early. That odd hush before the village decides what kind of day it's going to be. The sky hadn't made up its mind. The chairs were still stacked. The coffee hadn't brewed. Even the goat was quiet, for once.

Zorba arrived as he always had done, without ceremony, as if he'd simply stepped sideways out of history and into the present. He walked past the taverna. Past the beach. Past Spiros, who nodded once and then resumed pretending to stare at the sea. And then he stepped through the gate into the grove.

When Alex saw him, she froze.

Then she set down the lemon she was holding – gently, like it mattered – and followed him.

There was a steadiness to her step. Like someone stepping into a conversation she'd rehearsed in her mind, but never quite out loud.

I stayed back. Some moments don't need an audience.

Zorba stood in the centre, surrounded by trees we'd pruned and paths we'd carved. He looked around slowly – not just seeing, but measuring the present against memory. The string lights swayed overhead. The ground still bore the prints of last night's dinner. And under one of the lemon trees, a cat slept.

Then he turned to Alex.

Still no smile. Just that face carved out of stubbornness and salt.

Then he stared back at the grove, turning slowly in the golden light like he was seeing it for the first time – or maybe the last.

He let out a breath that felt like it had been waiting years to be released.

"You want the grove?" he said quietly. "It's yours."

Alex didn't answer at first. She couldn't. Her throat had tightened around whatever words might have been waiting. Instead, she nodded – just once – and looked at him the way you look at someone who's just handed you more than you know how to carry.

Zorba kept his gaze on the trees.

"They came again," he said. "The ones with folders and smiles. Offered me more than this place has seen in a decade.

Wanted to flatten the grove, pave it neat, put in glass walls and scented candles. A curated experience."

He snorted, softly.

"I told them no. Told them this place already has everything it needs – trees, people, *tsipouro*... and a goat with opinions."

Alex laughed, but her eyes were still glassy.

"You didn't even ask us," she said.

Zorba shrugged. "Didn't need to. You already answered. Every night you opened the doors. Every plate served. Every lemon picked."

He reached into his pocket, pulled out a folded envelope, and held it out to her.

"It's the deed to the lemon grove. Its official now," he said. "Signed. Stamped. Notarised by a man who owes me money and knows better than to argue."

Alex took it with both hands, like it might break.

"Take care of it," he said. "It remembers things."

And then, without waiting for thanks, he walked back towards the taverna, slow, steady, as if the weight he'd carried for years had finally shifted – but he paused at the edge of the grove.

"You already care for it. You gave it back its name. That's more than most." Then, just before turning to leave, he added, "Just don't turn it into a yoga retreat."

Alex let out a breath that was somewhere between a laugh and a sob. She tucked the envelope against her chest like a keepsake, not a contract. Katerina blinked in solemn approval from the shade.

It was done.

The grove was ours.

Not in the way land is bought and sold. Not in the way cities write deeds and banks demand forms. But in the way old fishermen pass on stories, and villages pass on responsibility: quietly, seriously, and always with love stitched into the silence.

We didn't announce it. There was no party. No toast. Just the usual rhythm.

The chairs came out.

The grill fired up.

Spiros took his place under the olive tree, exhaled slowly, and said nothing, which, in our village, meant everything.

And the lemon trees rustled in the morning light, like they'd always known this was how it would end.

With care.

With trust.

With Alex, holding a deed she hadn't asked for, to a place she'd already given her heart.

CHAPTER FORTY-NINE

A Place to Belong

I never thought I'd belong here.

Not really.

Not in that deep, bone-warming way you see in people born of a place. People like Spiros, who claim to remember storms from before the weather was named. People like Theodora, who can trace her grandmother's oregano patch to the centimetre and knows exactly how many eggs every chicken in the village should be laying in July.

I was the outsider. The one with the accent. The one who needed subtitles for family arguments and couldn't remember which saint went with which name day. The one who measured things in centimetres and inches instead of olives.

And yet...

As I stood in the grove that morning, the air heavy with sun and lemon blossom, I realised I hadn't felt like an outsider in a long time. I hadn't noticed when that had changed.

Maybe it was the day Spiros poured me the good *tsipouro* without comment. Maybe it was when Maria started gossiping about me in my presence instead of just outside the window. Or when Dimitri began greeting me with a grunt instead of suspicious silence.

Maybe it was just Alex.

Being with Alex means never standing still. She talks with her hands, cooks like she's feeding a wedding, and believes that chaos, when organised with care, is another form of harmony.

She taught me that Greek life isn't about control, it's about surrender. Not giving up. *Giving in.* To flavour, to feeling, to fire.

It's about knowing that nothing will start on time, someone will argue over the salt, and there's a good chance a goat will escape into the car park – and loving it anyway.

She showed me how to live here. Not as a visitor. But as someone who belongs.

The grove changed things. Not because we planted it – we didn't. Not because we earned it – not in the legal sense. But because we *listened* to it. Cared for it. Stepped gently where others had forgotten.

It gave us more than lemons and shade. It gave us *connection*.

To this village. To each other. To the strange, wonderful rhythm of Greek life, where nothing goes according to plan, but everything somehow works.

It taught us that land, like love, doesn't ask for a signature.

It asks for attention. And in giving it, you find something you didn't realise you'd been searching for.

The taverna still rattles when the wind comes in from the north.

The fridge still hums ominously.

Spiros still refuses to use the menu and insists that "the fish should speak for itself".

Nothing's perfect. But nothing should be. Because in this beautiful, crumbling, lemon-scented corner of Greece, we found something far better than peace and quiet.

We found *purpose*. We found friends. We found ourselves. We found a grove that doesn't belong to us but lets us belong to *it*.

And in that quiet belonging, between the grilled sardines, the bent chairs, the sea breeze, and the scent of thyme, we found home.

CHAPTER FIFTY

Under the Lemon Moon

We never planned a closing celebration. That would've made it sound like something was ending. But nothing ends in Telios. Things shift. Quietly, then suddenly. Like the sea changing direction or someone rearranging the chairs without asking.

Summer was winding down. The tourists were packing up their inflatables and heading home. And the taverna? It would return to what it had always been: a place for locals to meet, eat, argue, and forget what they were arguing about.

So it wasn't a farewell. It wasn't even a "season finale".

It was just… the next chapter. Slower. Quieter. Still full of feta. But tonight, we would dance.

No invitations were sent. No posters printed. It was just a night. A warm, windless, lemon-glow night.

One moment it was Tuesday. The next, Theodora was marinating lamb, Maria was painting signs that said "Table 7 reserved for good stories", and Spiros was stringing old fishing floats into lanterns without telling anyone why.

Claude brought candles. Eleni brought lemon soap as "thank you gifts", though most people thought they were cheese and took a bite.

George set up a cheese-tasting station that prompted a spirited debate over which feta had the most "emotional depth".

Alex hung the last row of lights from the olive tree to the fence, humming to herself.

And me?

I just stood there for a moment and watched. Watched the villagers shuffle in, arms full of food and stories. Watched the kids run through the grove like it was a forest from a forgotten fable. Watched Zorba take his usual seat and, for the first time in weeks, smile.

The table under the biggest lemon tree filled first. Then the one beside Spiros's bench.

Then the ones no one remembered bringing out. And before long, the grove was glowing.

There were grilled sardines.

Roasted aubergines.

Vassiliki's walnut cake that may or may not have caused three mild sugar-related outbursts.

Dimitri's latest "lemon-infused *tsipouro*" appeared in a bottle with no label and the strength of a small jet engine.

Music floated up from someone's speaker – *bouzouki, rembetika*, the occasional bout of nineties Greek pop that got more popular the later it got.

People danced.

Poorly. Proudly.

The kind of dancing where arms are flung out not because they know the step, but because they trust the earth to catch them.

Under the trees, with lemons still clinging to the branches and petals falling into wine glasses, something soft and wordless unfolded: this was a *homecoming*.

At one point, Zorba stood. Silence fell, as it does when the village patriarch moves without explanation.

He raised a glass, cleared his throat, and said, "You've done alright."

Which, in Greek village terms, is a standing ovation.

Then he sat back down and mumbled something about the lamb being slightly dry.

We took it as a blessing.

The night didn't end, not really.

People trickled home slowly, reluctantly, like sleepwalking poets trying not to wake the dream.

Alex and I were the last to leave. She walked the grove one more time, fingers brushing the branches. I picked up a dropped lemon, still warm from the sun and touched by the night air.

"It smells like a story," I said.

Alex smiled. "It is."

***

The grove is still there. It still doesn't really belong to us. But we belong to *it*. And in the end, that's what matters most. Not the title. Not the deed. But the shared table. The shouted laughs. The long walks. The crickets in the grass. The fact that, in a world full of broken things, this place, this tangled, glowing, lemon-scented patch of earth, somehow made us whole.

So if you ever find yourself in northern Evia, near a fishing village where the tables are a little uneven and the stories never end...

Pull up a chair. We've saved you a seat.

CHAPTER FIFTY-ONE

A Parthenon by the Sea

There is, on the edge of the harbour, a particular rock I like to sit on.

It's not impressive, nor especially smooth, but it faces the sea, catches the morning light, and has enough of a slope to lean back with a cup of coffee and watch the village wake up.

This morning, it was quiet.

The taverna, ours now, somehow, was not yet open. The tables were stacked; the chairs tilted like sleeping animals. The grove shimmered with leftover joy and lemon blossoms.

And as I sat on my rock, listening to the water lap against the quay, I thought about nothing and everything.

I've visited the real Parthenon a dozen times. Each time, I expect something grand. Something museum-perfect. And each time, it catches me off guard. Not because it's majestic, though it is, but because it's crooked.

None of the lines are straight. The columns lean. The marble ripples like water. The proportions aren't mathematical, they're emotional. Crafted not for perfect symmetry, but for perfect feeling. It's a temple built on illusion.

And yet, it remains more beautiful than any straight-lined thing I've ever seen.

And here, by the sea, our taverna is not a temple. It has missing tiles. The tables wobble.

We're still not sure if the electricity meets any known standard. We argued about the name.

We argued about the grill. We argued about the chairs, the signage, the olive oil supplier, and whether or not Claude should be allowed to paint a mural of Camus above the fridge.

But we did it. We opened. And the people came. And they stayed. They laughed. They shouted. They danced.

And somehow, out of the chaos, out of the *tsipouro*-soaked madness, came something that felt like home.

So here it is. Our little ruin. Our cracked, crooked, sun-bleached, lemon-scented sanctuary. The Parthenon by the sea. Not perfect. Not finished. Not easy. But alive. And loved.

The real Parthenon has weathered two thousand years of storms, invasions, earthquakes, gunpowder, and tourists with selfie sticks, and it still stands: wobbly, cracked, glorious.

And maybe that's what we're all trying to build. Something that lasts. Something that matters.

***

I don't know what happens next.

There will be more storms. More broken chairs. More laughter. More bureaucrats.

But I know this: if you're lucky, life gives you a place. Not to worship from afar, but to live in. To argue in. To cook in. To spill wine in.

A Parthenon not on a hill, but by the sea.

Built not of marble, but of mornings, and madness, and the kind of stubborn love that makes things grow: lemons, dreams, families.

Even if they lean a little in the wind.

The End… or perhaps just the next beginning.

EPILOGUE

AFTER THE STORM

The kitchen, once a battlefield, now smelled of thyme and liniment.

Chairs were crooked. Plates were empty. George had gone to lie down somewhere cool. Theodora was polishing a ladle like it had been through combat, which, to be fair, it had. And the rest of us were still counting spoons to make sure none had been taken as souvenirs or weapons.

That's when Alex found it.

Tucked beside the napkin holder, half-hidden under a stray crumb of *koulourakia*: a rosary. Wooden. Worn smooth by decades of faith and fingers. The kind your grandmother would use in church, in traffic, and during long conversations about your life choices.

No note. No name. Just the gentle presence of something sacred left behind.

"It was deliberate," said Father Evangelos, who had appeared as if summoned by the scent of spiritual residue. "They leave things sometimes. When they've been moved."

"Or when they're plotting something," said Alex.

He shrugged. "Same thing, really."

Mary picked it up reverently, set it on the shelf behind the counter, next to the olive oil and the emergency *raki*. A quiet shrine to chaos, holiness, and elderly ferocity.

But the rosary wasn't the only thing left behind.

Later that night, when we were wiping down the tables and pretending the fridge didn't sound like it was dying in Morse code, Theodora found something else.

A folded piece of paper.

Slipped into the cutlery drawer, carefully tucked between the forks and wisdom.

It was a recipe. Handwritten. In perfect, spidery script.

"*Dolmadakia tou Theou*" – vine leaves of the Lord. Instructions. Ingredients. Warnings. A final note: "Only make these when you truly forgive someone. Otherwise, they'll be bitter."

Theodora stared at it.

"Well?" I asked.

She didn't answer. She just folded it back up, slipped it into her apron pocket, and went back to stirring the soup.

We never found out who left it. No one returned to claim the rosary. No *yiayia* phoned to check on the missing beads. And no one mentioned the incident again.

But the next time dolmadakia appeared on the menu, they were softer. Richer. Forgiving.

And Theodora, just once, smiled while cooking.

We didn't ask why.

Because in Telios, you learn not to ask too many questions about the divine, the dead, or grandmothers with unfinished business.

You just eat the food.

And say thank you.

Even if no one's there to hear it.

And the story is just beginning.

Bonus chapter from

Zorba's Taverna: A Parthenon by the Sea

The Second Book in the Zorba Series

ZORBA'S TAVERNA

THE TROUBLE WITH GOATS & MAYORS

PETER BARBER

CHAPTER ONE

THE INVASION OF THE
SPOON-WIELDING MATRIARCHS

Here in Telios, we don't point at laminated menus or glossy photos of food that never quite look like the real thing. We certainly don't argue about who ordered what or demand separate bills with military precision. This is not that kind of place.

Running a taverna in a Greek village is like conducting an orchestra where every musician has a strong opinion and three of them brought goats. In winter, the customers are locals, bundled in layers, seeking warmth, gossip, and familiarity. They come not for a culinary experience, but for comfort. A seat. A story. A place to be.

Come summer, everything shifts. The tourists arrive. Sunburnt and slightly dazed, clutching guidebooks, sunscreen, and expectations. But here's the magic: we all share. The villagers don't mind. In fact, they enjoy it. Everyone ends up mixing: locals, visitors, old friends, strangers who become regulars. Conversation flows like wine. Someone always translates. Someone always laughs.

In Greek village tavernas, food is never just food. It's emotion. It's memory. It's a full-body, full-table experience.

We don't order individually here. You don't get your own plate of grilled meat while the person next to you eats their salad in isolation. That's not how this works. In the villages, a meal is a team sport.

Fish is ordered by the kilo. Salad comes in a bowl that could double as a birdbath. Dishes of potatoes, wild greens, grilled vegetables, and beans appear and settle in the middle of the table like old friends. Everyone reaches in. Everyone shares. There's no ceremony. No politeness required. If you want something, reach for it. Or point. Or ask loudly across the table.

It took time, and no small amount of intervention, to get our visitors to understand this. Especially early on, when we'd get orders like "two pork chops with fries" and "a small plate of spaghetti for the child". The kitchen would sigh. Theodora would raise an eyebrow so sharp it could slice aubergine.

And eventually, someone (usually Alex) would gently explain:

"No, my darling. You don't order for yourself. You order for the table."

At first, they resisted. We saw the panic in their eyes. The need for control. The fear of a rogue anchovy. But then, slowly, gloriously, they adjusted. They dipped their bread into communal *tzatziki*. They passed the octopus. They tried the mysterious green thing and liked it more than expected.

They relaxed.

Because this isn't just about efficiency. It's about trust. About being part of something, even if just for one meal. You learn that food, when shared, tastes better. Jokes land harder. Wine lasts longer. Strangers feel familiar.

We still have to gently re-educate the occasional stubborn tourist, the one who wants a gluten-free burger with no onion, no burger and no bun. But most? Most get it eventually. And when they do, they don't just eat.

They belong.

That's the Greek village way. Messy. Generous. Loud. And absolutely perfect.

***

But sometimes, just sometimes, we're tested to the very edge, and beyond.

Because not all tourists are wide-eyed and curious, ready to try something new. No. Occasionally, we get *the others*. The ones who already know *exactly* how Greek food should be. Because, according to them, their family *invented* it. Somewhere between the invention of democracy and baklava.

And when that tourist comes not alone, but in numbers – say, an entire *busload* of Greek grandmothers – well, that's not a visit. That's an inspection. A culinary inquisition. A cross-generational ambush with handbags and rolling pins.

They descend like a benevolent yet terrifying storm cloud, armed with opinions, embroidered handkerchiefs, and enough cooking expertise to host a twelve-part documentary on the History Channel. And they don't just eat.

They *judge*.

It began like all disasters do in Greece: quietly. With sunshine, good intentions, and a phone call that should have been a warning.

"A quick stop," the man said. "Just a bite," he promised. "A group of pilgrims," he added. "They've just come from Saint John the Russian."

Which, in retrospect, was the first red flag. Because anyone holy enough to survive a pilgrimage to Prokopi, and devout enough to schedule thermal baths after, wasn't coming here for a light lunch. They were coming for answers. And possibly vengeance.

What he didn't say was that the "group" consisted of 42 Athenian *yiayiades*. Each one with arthritis in the knees, righteousness in the bones, and at least three generations of culinary superiority flowing through their veins.

Zorba's taverna was about to receive the ultimate test.

The bus arrived with the energy of a Trojan horse. Doors hissed open. Feet descended. Umbrellas were unsheathed like bayonets. They came in floral prints, orthopaedic sandals, and expressions that could cause milk to curdle.

Alex appeared at the gate. "No," she said. Just that. Then she turned to Theodora. "Battle stations."

Inside, George calmly refilled the cheese drawer. Mary tied her hair back with the air of a woman about to charm or kill. Dimitri hid the octopus, not because it wasn't fresh, but because he feared for its soul.

Claude ran off to hang bunting. Eleni reached for her strongest stamp. I, naturally, grabbed a pen. Useless in a fight, but excellent for recording the casualties.

The first *yiayia* entered. Marched past the tables. Walked straight into the kitchen.

No hellos. Just a sniff and a narrowed eye.

"Where is the ladle?" she asked.

Theodora, already seething, pointed. "In my hand."

Another arrived. "Why is the grill cold?"

"It's not," said George, already turning it up.

The floodgates opened. One by one, they entered the sacred kitchen space. Theodora's realm. Our temple. Within minutes it had become a battleground of conflicting wisdom and passive-aggressive expertise.

"This oregano is tired." "Who taught you to salt beans like that?" "My cousin's daughter's neighbour is a chef in Piraeus, and even she wouldn't dare boil this cabbage."

One leaned into a pot, sniffed deeply, and said, "Too much onion." Another leaned into the same pot two minutes later: "Not enough onion."

Theodora didn't flinch. She simply turned to George and muttered, "I'm going to jail today."

Meanwhile, Mary tried to steer the rest toward the tables with her usual weapon of choice: grace.

"Would you like to sit, *kyria*?" she offered sweetly.

"I'll sit when I see the fish," came the reply.

Dimitri burst into the taverna with the theatrical flair of a man delivering a national treasure, lugging a crate of the day's catch as though he'd just heroically plucked it straight from Poseidon's beard. He was glistening with seawater, sweat, and misplaced confidence.

The Athens *yiayias*, all forty-three of them, armed with handbags, prayer beads, and weaponised opinions, immediately swarmed around him like piranhas in floral cardigans.

He set the crate down with a grunt. "Fresh from the rocks," he declared. "Still dreaming of the sea."

One yiayia leaned in. "That one's cloudy-eyed."

"Cloudy? It's soulful!" Dimitri insisted.

Another poked a silver specimen with a crucifix. "Looks like it died of embarrassment."

A third *yiayia*, whose earrings could pick up satellite channels, sniffed loudly. "You call this a red mullet? I've seen redder faces at funerals."

Dimitri's grin faltered.

One particularly fierce granny, wielding a lace fan like a judge's gavel, pointed to a bream. "This one's bloated. You leave it too long in the sun?"

"No! It's just… robust," Dimitri offered weakly.

"They smell wrong," someone muttered.

"Smells fine to me," said Dimitri, sniffing a sea bass defensively.

"Are you sure they're fresh, *koumparé*?" came the reply.

"They were swimming this morning!"

"Towards what? A sewer?"

"Back in my day," one *yiayia* announced, arms crossed like a general, "you'd never serve this in a house with dignity. We'd have thrown it to the cat."

The cat wandered past, sniffed the crate, and left silently. It was devastating.

They picked through the crate like forensic inspectors at a crime scene. Tails were lifted, gills examined, tiny fish interrogated for their culinary intentions.

One pulled out what might have been a sardine. "What's this one even trying to be?"

"A lesson," said her friend.

And then, with a communal sigh of dismay and the

solemnity of a church committee about to reject a bake sale, they turned to Dimitri.

"Young man," said the eldest, adjusting her orthopaedic sandals, "go back to the sea. Apologise to it."

By the time they moved on to critiquing the kitchen knives, Dimitri was muttering to himself in the corner, nursing a bruised ego and possibly a *tsipouro*.

Most of the fish were quietly sent to the back of the kitchen, their fate postponed.

And the *yiayias*? They made their way behind the counter, sleeves rolled, opinions sharpened.

One brought out a lemon and held it up dramatically. "Did you pick this in anger?"

Claude arrived with a jug of wine and said something poetic about Dionysus. One of them slapped his hand away from the olives and told him not to waste time talking when the *tzatziki* still needed straining.

Zorba didn't move. He sat by the door, arms folded, one eyebrow arched in a way that suggested he'd seen wars with fewer casualties.

Father Evangelos was summoned to "bless the kitchen before someone swears". He arrived, saw the chaos, and promptly blessed himself.

The kitchen now had nine active cooks, three arguing over whether lentils needed mint, one restocking the fridge, and two demanding access to the storeroom "just to see the potatoes".

Theodora defended the pans like a lioness defending her cubs. George guarded the feta.

Alex tried to restore order.

"Theodora runs this kitchen!" she shouted.

"No, she *organises* it," a *yiayia* corrected. "Running requires soul."

And then, from somewhere near the sink: "The spirit of your moussaka is willing. But your béchamel is weak."

Outside, the tables groaned under the weight of unsolicited wisdom. *Yiayiades* were shouting across the terrace in the universal language of culinary judgment:

"Did you see the rice?"

"It was trembling."

"Too much salt. Or too little. Depends how much you care about your arteries."

"I had a dream once where the *pastitsio* was perfect. This is not that dream."

And yet, they ate.

Every bite came with commentary. Every swallow with a side of advice. And every glance toward the kitchen with the expectation of repentance.

But then came dessert.

Vassiliki, quiet until now, emerged with her tray of *galaktoboureko* like an ancient priestess revealing the oracle. She said nothing, but just placed it gently on the table.

One *yiayia* spooned a bite into her mouth. Paused.

"My grandmother made it like this," she said softly.

The others stopped. Tasted. Remembered.

"I was a child again," someone whispered. "In Kalamata. Before the war."

Silence descended.

Then: "You used semolina, didn't you?"

"Yes," said Vassiliki.

"Good," the woman said. "Otherwise, I'd have to kill you."

They left as they came – loud, opinionated, floral – but somehow healed. Whether it was the food, the laughter, or the brief skirmish over the olive oil, no one could say. But as the bus disappeared in a cloud of dust and eucalyptus rub, the taverna exhaled.

Theodora leaned on the counter. "If I ever see another floral handbag in my kitchen–"

George handed her a biscuit.

Alex flopped into a chair.

"They stormed us," she muttered.

"And we fed them," I said.

"Barely."

Zorba stood, stretched, and said simply, "Now you're ready."

"For what?" asked Mary.

"For everything," he replied.

And we believed him.

Because if you can survive a bus full of grandmothers, you can survive anything. Even the tourism board.

Acknowledgements

A Goat, a Godmother, and The Girl Who Made It All Possible

Every book is a collaboration. Some people contribute with edits, others with stories, some just by living in a way so gloriously impossible to ignore that I had no choice but to write them down.

But this one, this slightly ridiculous, deeply joyful, occasionally goat-interrupted tale, starts and ends with one person.

To Alex, you are my compass and my map. My sun and my occasional storm. You didn't just walk with me into this village, you dragged me through bureaucracy, danced me through chaos, and handed me a taverna-shaped dream with a look that said, "Of course we can."

You taught me that dreams don't come with planning permission. That love, like Greece, is best when it's loud, unapologetic, and occasionally on fire. That family is chosen as much as it's inherited. That home is where the sea meets your stubbornness.

And yes, I built you a Parthenon.

But you? You built this life.

You are the heroine of every story in this book, whether or not your name is mentioned. And if I have done any of this justice, it is only because I had the honour of watching you – fierce, funny, fearless – bring a me, and a forgotten lemon grove, back to life.

Now, to the rest of the village. You know who you are. Or at least, you'll pretend not to.

To *Maria*, for proving that gossip is not only faster than light, but sometimes the glue that holds a village together.

To *George*, for sharing his cheese, his silence, and the quiet kind of strength that never asks to be noticed.

To *Theodora*, for feeding us fiercely, judging us accurately, and reminding us that love often comes seasoned with oregano and served with a warning.

To *Mary*, for carrying trays, tempers, and the spirit of the village with effortless grace, and for letting us all believe we were better behaved than we were.

To *Stamos*, for showing up, fixing things we didn't know were broken, and reminding us that chaos is just another form of craftsmanship.

To *Dimitri,* for the fish, the firewood, the folklore, and for never once asking for anything in return but a decent drink and a good argument.

To *Spiros,* for sitting exactly where he always has, anchoring the village in place with one scowl, one glass, and decades of knowing better.

To *Claude,* for the poetry, the tablecloths, the accidental anarchy – and for making us believe, if only briefly, that jazz nights might be a good idea.

To *Eleni,* for turning bureaucracy into performance art and protecting us from paperwork with the ferocity of a lioness with a stamp.

To *Vassiliki,* for baking peace into every pie and turning pastries into a form of diplomacy the UN could only dream of.

To *Father Evangelos,* for blessing what needed blessing, ignoring what needed ignoring, and always knowing the difference.

And of course, to *Katerina* the goat, for teaching us that family can be loud, demanding, occasionally destructive, and still entirely worth it. She reminded us that love isn't tidy – it climbs fences, eats your laundry, and follows you home whether you like it or not.

To *Zorba,* wherever you are, leaning against a sun-warmed wall with a glass in hand, thank you. For the table, the stories, the taverna, and the trust. For letting go and letting us try.

And to *Greece*. For your wildness, your warmth, your utterly illogical perfection. For cracked paths and ancient songs. For the sea that never stops arguing with the shore. For nights filled with laughter, fireworks, lemon-scented chaos, and the occasional bureaucratic emergency.

You are the reason I write. The reason I stay. The reason I keep building Parthenons where no one asked for them.

(And at this point, a quick pause for an important tribute.)

This book – chaotic, meandering, occasionally held together with olive pits and optimism – would not exist in anything like its current form without Debbie Chapman.

Debbie, my editor, somehow possesses the rare gift of a photographic memory and infinite patience. She can recall the exact number of times I've used the word "chaos" (too many), where I first described a lemon tree as "militant", and whether I've already had Dimitri throw a fish in Chapter Three or Chapter Nine. She sees everything. Even the commas I tried to hide.

She has joined forces, against all odds, with a writer who has the attention span of a sunburnt goldfish and the file-management system of a distracted squirrel. While I ping between ideas, chapters, and time zones, she gently – and miraculously – turns it all into a book. Not just any book, but one that somehow makes sense, flows, and even has consistent spelling. (A feature my early drafts strongly opposed.)

More than an editor, she's become a creative partner and friend – someone who understands the rhythm of the village, the voices of these people, and, most terrifyingly of all, *me*.

Thank you, Debbie. You've made this story stronger, funnier, and far more human.

And you even let me keep the goat jokes. Now that's love.

And to you, dear reader. Thank you for pulling up a wobbly chair at our uneven table, for listening, for laughing, for believing, even just for a moment, that life might be found in a taverna by the sea, with too much feta and not enough formality.

NOW RAISE YOUR GLASS.

To love. To laughter.
To Alex.
And to the goat.
With all my heart,

Peter Barber

About the Author

Peter Barber is the award-winning author of the *Parthenon and Zorba's Taverna* series, humorous, heartfelt explorations of Greek village life that have delighted readers around the world.

A British native who traded drizzle for sunlight, Peter swapped the grey skies of England for the blue horizons of Greece, and in doing so, found not only a new home but a new voice. His books capture the irresistible mix of beauty, chaos, and humanity that defines Greek life, told with the dry wit of an Englishman trying (and mostly failing) to stay sensible in a country where nothing ever goes to plan, and somehow that's the charm.

The *Parthenon trilogy*, *A Parthenon on Our Roof*, *A Parthenon in Pefki*, and *The Parthenon Paradox*, introduced readers to Peter's world: a British outsider lovingly absorbed into a village that runs on rumour, tsipouro, and eternal optimism. At the heart of it all stands Alex, his fiery, fiercely Greek wife, part muse, part hurricane, whose influence has turned his quiet English logic into something far more entertaining.

Now, in his new *Zorba's* series, Peter returns to the same world, a fictionalised village inspired by real life in North Evia, to tell a broader story of community, hope, and the absurd heroism of everyday people. *Zorba's Parthenon: A Taverna by the Sea* follows the fight to save a beloved taverna from red tape, developers, and fate itself. It's a tale of laughter, loyalty, and the unbreakable bond between a village and the sea, a (mostly) true story about stubborn love and comic resistance.

Blending memoir and fiction, Barber's writing has been praised for its warmth, vivid characters, and the ease with which it finds humour in the tragic and meaning in the ridiculous. His books are a tribute to Greece, its food, its spirit, its contradictions, and to the people who remind us that paradise is rarely perfect, but always worth fighting for.

When he's not writing, Peter divides his time between Greece and the UK, where he claims to be working but is often found in a village café "researching dialogue." He continues to find inspiration in the laughter, gossip, and good chaos of his adopted home.

Whether you've lived in Greece, fallen in love there, or simply dream of escaping to a sunlit terrace overlooking the sea, Peter's books will make you laugh, sigh, and perhaps understand a little more about the stubborn joy of living.

The Zorba's Taverna series celebrates what Peter does best, finding comedy in catastrophe, poetry in everyday life, and humanity in all its noisy, glorious imperfection.

Find out more at:

https://peterbarberwriter.com/

Social Media:

Author Page
https://www.facebook.com/AuthorPeterBarber/

Writing about Greece:
https://www.facebook.com/groups/369010324939088